COLLECTING HOUSES

for my carpenter son Elisha —
who understands how to
listen to the language of
a house —
Love, Mum   2003

COLLECTING HOUSES

17th Century Houses

20th Century

Adventures

ANNE W. BAKER

To order additional copies of this book, contact:
Xlibris Corporation
1-888-795-4274
www.Xlibris.com
Orders@Xlibris.com
20134

Contents

FOR MY CHILDREN

Will, Harriet, Abby, Elisha, Nicole, Ben, Sarah.

So many people and so many houses influenced the writing of this book that it is impossible to mention them all. But I want to give special thanks to:

Steve Tyson for sharing his old house soul; Doug Keffer for his unfailing loyalty;

Charles Cann for his perfect drawings of the Mott House; Gretchen and Barry Mazer for teaching me the magic of words; Rodie Siegler for reading and rereading the drafts;

Gail Pool for her straightforward advise; and Clara Stites for teasing this manuscript into shape.

For God's sake, what am I after?
Some treasure, or tiny garden?
Or that untrodden place,
The house's very soul,
Where time has stored our footbeats
And the long skein of our voices?

Richard Wilbur.
From "A Hole In the Floor"

The Big House

I thought the only thing old about the house was my grandmother. She lived at the top of the hill next to the old Post Road in Wakefield, Rhode Island. My father called it the Big House. During the summers we lived at the bottom of the hill in the Little House. On rainy afternoons my mother would send me to the Big House to keep me out of trouble. I was a tomboy.

I can see myself then, maybe four or five, small and skinny with straight bobbed hair, dressed in blue shorts and a blue and white striped T-shirt. I had four matching sets, each a different color. They had come in a box from Best & Company. My mother called them coordinates, but sometimes I got the colors mixed up. After she made sure that I had the blues with the blues or the yellows with the yellows, she'd tell me to go straight to the Big House, and as I started up the lane, she would holler, "Mind your manners and for heavens sakes stay clean."

*   *   *

My grandmother didn't call her house the Big House, she called it the farmhouse, but I knew she was mistaken, and so were my parents. It looked like a castle I'd seen in a book. There were archways to drive through, porches on all sides to keep the castle company, and giant stone steps that led up to the kitchen, a kitchen that always smelled of oatmeal cookies. The cook would hand me one and then she'd say, "Go on now, your Granny is waiting."

The only way out of the kitchen was through a pantry filled with plates, bowls and teapots that rattled with each of my footsteps as if the china was talking. At the far end was a door with a round glass window. I would stand on my tiptoes, look through the window, then slowly push the door open and peek around the corner. If nothing moved, I would scurry through the dark space to get to the stairs leading to the second floor and my grandmother.

She called it her solarium, a room where she spent her afternoons lounging on a wicker settee, her grown-up body outlined by cushions embroidered with laughing flowers, while a crackling soap opera talked make-believe beside her. Her hair was like a silver cloud hovering over a landscape of hills and valleys, and her chins lay on her *Peter Pan* collar like pillowy fields.

After I kissed her turned up check, she would tell me to sit down and be quiet. I never knew what chair to sit in. They were scattered all around. My grandmother told me not to move them. "They're protecting the old floor boards," she would say.

But I was sure she'd been playing musical chairs and didn't want me to know. Sometimes she would doze off and that's when I would explore the many dark and mysterious rooms in her house, rooms that creaked and groaned, and were so tilted I would pretend I was sailing a ship in a storm.

Sometimes I spent the night in the Big House, and my grandmother and I would eat in the dining room, a room I was sure was her throne room and the table in the middle, sparkling with candlelight, her throne. I'd pretend the big fireplace at the end of the room was where her army hid, the wooden posts in each corner were the sentry boxes for her guards, and the rows of wooden beams in the ceiling, a stockade to keep the Indians out.

After we sat down, my grandmother would shake a tiny silver bell and like magic food would appear on the table. The lamb chops came with white knee socks, the beans with jackets of butter, and the mashed potatoes sprinkled with parsley were piled on my plate like a hat. I wanted to ask her if this was the same uniform the guards in the sentry boxes wore. But my grandmother and I never talked much.

* * *

In 1941, when I was twelve, I found a photograph album in my grandmother's attic. Its thick black covers were hinged together with ribbon, and stamped on the front in gold letters was the name *Matunuck Brook Farm*. Curious, I sat down on the floor, opened the cover, and leafed through the coarse black pages. Faded chocolate colored photographs were held in place by little black triangles. Below each picture, written in fancy script and white ink, were the names of the people. I remember the delicious feeling of ages ago creeping out as I turned each page—ladies with croquet mallets, men with pitchforks or straw hats and moustaches, women in long dresses and big bonnets, and fat babies in wicker carriages. Sometimes people wore summer clothes, sometimes fur coats. Sometimes a person sat in a horse-drawn carriage or wrapped in a blanket in a sleigh, but the people were always next to my grandmother's house, as if they were part of the house and the house part of them.

The last three photographs were pictures of houses. The first I recognized as my grandmother's house, but I wondered why *1890—After the Additions* was written underneath. Nobody had told me that additions had been added.

The middle photograph also said *Matunuck Brook Farm*, but it showed a two story house with a lean-to and the date 1851. This seemed strange; it didn't look like my grandmother's house. I was sure somebody had made a mistake.

The last was a muted and fuzzy photograph of a painting. *Matunuck Brook Farm—1690*, was written below it. Now I was really confused. This was a picture of a tiny house with a big chimney. No way could these three houses be one and the same.

I looked back and forth, from one to the next, hoping to find an answer, and then I realized that the top of the chimney matched in all three. Bewildered, I took the album downstairs and showed my grandmother. "Is this really true? This house was built in 1690?"

"Oh yes," she said. "This living room is part of the original house," and she pointed to a beam in the middle of the ceiling. "That's all that shows now. The rest is hidden behind the walls."

I must have looked perplexed because she hugged me and said, "Don't worry, give it time and you too will find out a house has a life of its own."

*   *   *

Busy growing up, I didn't see my grandmother too often after that. Then, at the age of fourteen, I was sent away to boarding school. Anyway that's what my mother called it, but when I arrived I soon found out it was really a place one is sent to be overhauled. I knew how to drive a tractor, use my father's tools, build a clubhouse, and hit a bull's-eye with my rifle—skills my mother thought neither attractive nor appropriate for a young lady. I hated the school. I didn't want to be stuck with a lot of girls, told how to sip tea and cross my ankles. I felt as though I was being washed in a detergent, and when hung out to dry I'd be like everybody else. I refused to conform and graduated at the bottom of my class with no more skills than those I had acquired growing up as a tomboy. I didn't know then how important these skills would become to me.

I had reached the age of eighteen, a number that's supposed to bring magic, but I wasn't college material and the only magical thing in my life was a love affair with a guy who thought we should get married and have babies. He told me he loved me for who I was. Getting married seemed like the right decision.

We moved into an apartment in Providence, but after a year we realized that neither of us wanted to live in the city. We looked for land in the country. In East Greenwich, Rhode Island, we found a wooded lot on Pojac Point, with a knoll overlooking the Potowomut River. A perfect spot to build a house. Too young to know what kind of house we wanted, we hired an architect who designed and built a redwood sided, one story house with a flat roof. The design, he told us, was the up-and-coming thing for the 50s, except it looked like the box a house might have come in, not like a house that could put down roots like my grandmother's house.

It didn't act like any other house I knew either. The flat roof, designed to hold water for insulation, leaked in the summer, and in the winter, when the water froze, the ice cracked with such a loud noise that the first time I heard it I thought a UFO had landed. The walls were windows from ceiling to floor, to capture the solar heat. The floors were slabs of cement, to hold the hot water pipes for the inside heat. An outside thermostat was supposed to warn the floors when the sun would be in charge of heating the house. Except the sun and the hot water pipes always disagreed—the house was often one hundred degrees—and I'd spend the winter in my bathing suit with the doors wide open.

All the furniture was built in, and when my grandmother came to visit her only comment was, "Well at least when you move, you'll have nothing to take except your children."

* * *

Five children later, we finally outgrew the house. It was time to look for something more closely resembling a mansion, a need that coincided with my grandmother's death and the astonishing news that she'd left me her house of twenty-two rooms. Apparently I was the only one in my family who had ever shown any interest in her house.

The day we moved, I wasn't thinking that the house had been built in 1690, or that it had been in our family ever since, or even how glad I was to move back to Matunuck, the little town where I'd grown up. I was only thinking about the delicious amount of extravagant space. There were so many rooms each child could have three.

But once we were settled, I realized the kitchen, designed for a butler, a maid and a cook, was far from efficient for a mother of five. We didn't need a butler's pantry, a maid's pantry, or a room for flower arranging. We needed only a kitchen large enough to fit a family of seven.

One morning I woke up and decided it was time to tackle the kitchen. My husband, a nine-to-fiver, would be gone all day, and my children would be in school, so with the hours that were mine and the confidence of my tomboy skills, I began. As chunks of plaster and sections of sheet rock succumbed to my wrecking bar, the past, now awakened, escaped to lounge as dust throughout the house. I stared in awe at the things that had been sealed behind the walls: a fireplace bigger than a sofa, ancient paneling reused for patching, a patch where a door used to be, a Victorian black bathing suit stuffed in a crack, a broken teacup, a pewter candlestick, a leather shoe, a cast-iron cooking pot, bottles and buttons and all kinds of unfamiliar things.

Plaster, lath, stones and bricks filled the corners of the kitchen and dirt was everywhere, but I had such a feeling of euphoria that I pulled down the ceiling. When the dust cleared, I was delighted to see that the ceiling had hand planed joists the color of ebony—blackened from the years when they had been exposed. After I cleaned up the mess and looked at my discoveries, I smiled. This was what my grandmother meant when she said, "A house has a life of its own."

By the time my husband came home, the wreckage had gone beyond words, and when he proposed hiring a contractor to put it back the way it was, I was horrified. Granted, the only parts of the kitchen still functioning were the stove and the sink. The plaster had gaping holes, the fireplace looked like an incinerator, dishes were stacked on the floor, dirt was in the sugar bowl, and electric wires dangled from the ceiling.

Obviously something had to be done. But now that I had released the earliest days of the house, sealing them away again was out of the question, and I locked the doors against the threat of arriving carpenters.

I needed time to digest what I'd uncovered, decide how to combine the 17th century with the present, and then convince my husband how important it was to have the ancient parts of this house be part of our lives. It was easy to imagine my family gathered around the huge fireplace sharing its warmth while we watched the light from its flames dance on the ancient woodwork—except there wasn't any ancient woodwork.

Only the fireplace and the ceiling of exposed joists had survived two and a half centuries of renovations. The doors were modern, the floor was plywood, the wainscoting had disappeared, and there were only marks on the wall where shelves had been. If I could find some old doors, wainscoting and shelves to put back, this could be the room I imagined for my family. I explained this to my husband, and he agreed to call off the carpenters—at least for the present.

As far as I knew, salvage yards for antique house parts didn't exist in the 50s, but it occurred to me I could find the woodwork I needed in abandoned houses. I had seen empty houses when I was a teenager arrowhead hunting with my uncle in the woods of South County. We had used topographical maps as a guide to find Indian sites. The maps showed hills and valleys, streams and ponds, roads and trails but also a † for cemeteries and a ■ for houses—just what I needed.

I bought a map of Exeter, Rhode Island, one town over, an area where the roads were unpaved, the land was poor, and rumor had it that years ago many of the farmers had gone West in search of gold. This meant deserted houses. I rolled out the map looking for the mark of a house, especially one with a cemetery, a good indication the house had been around for at least a few generations. Widow Sweet Road caught my attention. I liked the name. It felt as if it had a past. I ran my pencil along the black line on the map and stopped at a ■ with a † —a house with a cemetery. The house was located at the end of a long lane and maybe forgotten. I put a big X on the spot, got into my convertible and with the map beside me headed out.

Once I arrived in the area, it didn't take long to find Widow Sweet Road or the gate posts that pinpointed the entrance to the lane I had marked with an X. I turned in. Pine, cherry and maple trees, a forested hall thick with branches, instantly smothered my car. I slowly drove forward, my vision blurred as if I was in a car wash being flailed by brushes. A fluttery, racing sensation churned in my stomach. I wondered where I'd end up, if I could turn around or what I'd say if I got caught. "Is Widow Sweet home?" just wouldn't work.

Time felt like forever before I finally came to a clearing and saw a house—the first thin wedge of civilization. I parked, grabbed a flashlight and got out of the car. What had been a front yard was a tangle of blueberry bushes, wild roses and honeysuckle. Wrestling my way under and over, I reached the doorway and looked in. The only inhabitant was a maple tree—its scrawny branches trying to reach the sunlight that spilled through a hole rotted in the roof. I stepped in, and hugging the walls I worked my way around the room. A few bits of pottery were scattered about, a broken chair leaned against a window, and a wooden box in the shape of a coffin lay in a corner. But the tiny stairway to the loft, the row of wooden pegs for hanging a shawl, and the back doorway that led to a kitchen garden told me this house had once been cozy. Shutting my eyes I could almost imagine Widow Sweet living here—the little kitchen tidy, the woodwork polished, the lace curtains billowing in the summer breeze as she sat by the window waiting for her husband who never returned. Killed in a war or crushed in a gold mine? Perhaps in his absence she had become a midwife. That would explain why the road bore her name—her location important for those who might need her, day or night.

I shook my head to break the spell, rolled over the coffin shaped box, and to my surprise found it was an old cupboard. The top half had three open shelves. The bottom half had a paneled door with its H-hinges still intact. It was absolutely perfect for my kitchen. I dragged the cupboard outside, put down the top of my convertible, laid the cupboard across the seat, and tied it to the door handle. I looked back at the house. Was I stealing, or was I rescuing, or was this no different than taking an arrowhead? On the other hand, if I left the cupboard there, it would rot to nothing. Certainly Widow Sweet would be pleased, I reasoned. So would my kitchen.

As soon as I arrived home, I filled a pail with warm soapy water and scrubbed away the mold and dirt on the cupboard. As it dried in the sun, I could see I had a treasure. The wood was pine. It had never been painted, and the little door had turned the color of toffee from being touched over and over again. I oiled and buffed the surface, and when I was done it glowed with the richness of a museum piece. Easing the cupboard into the kitchen, I propped it in a corner, put dishes on the shelves, and stood back to take a look. The cupboard belonged, as if part of the house right from the beginning.

Having found one derelict house, I went searching for more, the next day and the next, and for days after that. Using the map, I was becoming an expert on how and where to find them. And I kept discovering ancient houses sinking into the ground. The Great Depression of the 30s had driven people to the cities, and the houses, left alone, had given up the struggle against the grasses, the rain and the sun.

The ruins were often too far gone to show what the house had looked like, but buried underneath the rubble was material still able to speak for the past: floor boards worn thin by footsteps, doors that had provided privacy, pantry shelves that held necessities, and wall boards that had separated rooms. In a way that I didn't understand yet, I felt connected to the craftsman who had built the house and to the people who had lived in it. I fell in love with crooked stairs, rain soaked floors, rusty hardware, paint peeling doors, the mystery of it all. And I rescued whatever I could fit into my car. Stealing did not enter my mind. These were abandoned architectural foundlings that had to be saved.

Now that I had enough material, I tackled my kitchen. No, I wasn't a skilled carpenter, but I certainly didn't want any outsiders touching my treasures. Anyway I knew how to use tools and by taking woodwork out of a house I was learning how to put it back in. I was proud of the room and proud of myself as I saw how quickly the pieces I'd installed— wainscoting, shelving, doors, and the corner cupboard— blended with the original hand planed ceiling joists and huge stone fireplace.

The past had joined the 20th century. I knew that a life dedicated to the study and preservation of our architectural heritage had just begun.

Trespassing

For the fourth morning in a row, my husband told me I'd been house talking in my sleep. I couldn't remember what I'd been dreaming, but I'd wager it had something to do with trespassing. I was continuing to discover house ruins, and, although I didn't know why yet, I had to poke and prod in every one of them and save whatever I could. So yes, I was trespassing. But how could I find an owner before I found a house? I needed credentials—something to show I was innocent. Well, almost innocent.

I decided it might be useful if I carried a book I owned named *Old Houses of South County*. It was filled with pictures of old houses in my area, and if I was found trespassing I could whip it out, show the pictures, and simply explain that I was researching old houses—an approach that turned out to have extraordinary power. The few times I was happened upon, not only was the owner fascinated by the pictures, but I would be given permission to explore the wreckage and take whatever I wanted. But not always.

One day, driving down Biscuit City Road, a back road in South Kingston, Rhode Island, I spotted a chimney at the far end of a field. Naturally I had to stop for a better look. As I walked closer, I could see that the roof, floors, and some of the walls had collapsed into the cellar. I climbed down into the hole and shuffled through the mound of old wood. Parts of the house—shelving, a mantle, a door, a stairway, and all sorts of other pieces of woodwork—had slipped into the hole with hardly a scratch. I shuddered at the thought of the destruction if the chimney had fallen in also, but, thank God, it still looked as strong and as straight as when first built. I looked up to thank it for behaving and was surprised to see a raised-panel over-mantle still attached to its second floor fireplace. Deprived of shelter, the paneling, once a focal point of the room, now had the lonely look of somebody forgotten.

Absorbed in thinking of ways to rescue it, I jumped when I heard a voice. Looking behind me, I saw an old woman standing on the rim of the cellar, her small gnarled body silhouetted by the sun. One hand clutched a wicker basket and the other a cane. A long black skirt and tattered shawl gave her an ancient look, and for a moment I thought she had risen out of the surrounding shambles. She spoke, and her voice was angry. "What do you think you're doing?" she said.

I grabbed my backpack, climbed out of the cellar, pulled out the book, *Old Houses of South County*, and opened the cover—poised to give my spiel. But she would have none of it. Her only words—"Get out."

Chastened, I apologized for trespassing, stuck the book under my arm and walked back to my car. A tall man, his hands jammed into the pockets of his lumberman's jacket, was advancing towards me with an assertive stride, and I couldn't help thinking, "Now I'm in trouble." But as I got closer I could see his features held humor and tenderness. His bushy mustache and thick hair were marshmallow white, his eyes a milky blue, and there was a tilt to his head that reminded me of my grandfather about to spin a tale.

He nodded and in a friendly voice said, "Good morning," then asked if I had seen his wife. I told him there was a woman with a basket back at the house.

"Augh, she's gathering more wood," he sighed, half to himself. What he meant by gathering wood hadn't yet registered. I asked him if he owned the house.

"My wife does," he said, "It's been in her family for three hundred years," and he pointed to the knoll where her ancestors lay. He explained that he and his wife lived across the road, in the house with the *Honey for Sale* sign, and that each day his wife chopped up bits of wood from the old house and carried them home in her basket to burn in their stove.

"Here she comes now," he said.

My God, I thought, that's what he meant by gathering wood. She's burning up the house piece by piece.

I turned. She was walking up the lane, her basket full. I thought about trying to talk to her again. I wanted so badly to tell her that my only interest was in looking at the ruins, and with her permission, to save some of its pieces, but when she came closer her cracked lips twisted in scorn. Clearly further words would only antagonize her.

I gave her a few weeks to forget she'd ever seen me. Then with the excuse of buying honey, I made another visit. As I talked with her husband about the weather and his bees, she eyed me with an icy glare. She remembered, and I knew I'd have to work harder to earn my way in.

Over the fall and into the winter, with the pretext of buying honey, I visited again and again, each time nudging the conversation closer to talking about old houses. After five visits and as many jars of honey, she finally warmed up, surprising me by asking me into her house.

The icy ground crunched under my feet as she led me across the yard and through the rickety shed attached to the house. Dodging pails, swarm boxes, strainers, and a honey extractor, I followed her through a door and into the kitchen—a tiny kitchen, stale with a film of dusty sunlight. The only furniture was a corner cupboard, a maple table stacked with jars of honey, a rocking chair draped with a crocheted blanket, and a milking stool placed next to a fireplace. She handed me a jar of honey and pointed to the stool. I sat down. But when I realized she was rekindling the embers with chopped up bits of paneling, I froze. She threw on more pieces, and as the flames crackled with ancient sounds I had to suppress the awful thought that I was being warmed by the parts of her house. I said nothing, and she said nothing, and we continued to stare at the fire. Out of the flames came an agreement.

Handing me a pencil and paper she said, "Take whatever you want out of the house, but put down in writing that we're not responsible if you get hurt."

It had been six months, but worth the wait. While rescuing the fireplace paneling, some doors and shelving, I noticed that several of the framing timbers had moldings cut into their edges. I didn't know then that this type of treatment was named chamfering or that I was standing in the remains of a 17th century house. But I did have a powerful feeling that I had reached back into a past of which I knew nothing, a past that could be disappearing.

*　*　*

If I was going to add timbers to my rescue operations, I definitely needed something more practical for hauling than the convertible my father had given me. Every year he gave me a new one. He owned an automobile company, and he reasoned that my blond hair blowing in the wind as I cruised down the highway in a shiny new Ford was good advertisement. Definitely a nice arrangement for me until I started lugging home pieces of houses.

One day I said to my father, "Now that I have children, isn't it time to advertise a family?" The next car he gave me was a station wagon. Fortunately he didn't realize that the "family" would be house parts, tied to the top and spilling out the back.

The barn that had come with my grandmother's house was overflowing with mantles, chimney breasts and doors—two-panel, four-panel, eight-panel, board-and batten, and cupboard doors—plus wainscoting, baseboards, shelf boards, wall boards, beam casing, hardware. Now there were even pieces of post and beam frames.

For a while, I was perfectly content just sorting, studying, and talking to my collection. I was intrigued by the layers of paint in a series of colors leading back to the first brush stroke; by geometric designs scratched on the surface as if a traveling salesman had been selling compasses; by handmade nails; by ship-lapped or feather edged boards; by hinges shaped like an H, or an HL; and especially by the way a door was assembled without nails or glue, just little pegs to hold its mortises and tenons. I knew each piece like a friend. I knew what house each piece had come from, and I talked to all of them.

But there was so much I didn't know—things like how to date different types of framing, why timbers were sometimes left exposed and decorated and at other times covered with a beaded board, why some walls were studded and others vertically boarded. And I particularly wanted to understand about the types of joinery that held the frame of a house together. It was time to get to the books.

When I asked the librarian at my local library for books on architecture, she directed me to a shelf in the back of the room. It didn't take long before a leather-bound book caught my attention. Written on its spine was *Early Rhode Island Houses*. I pulled it out and opened the faded maroon cover. The book had been published in 1895 and the author was Norman Isham. As I scanned the pages, I realized that this was a study of 17th century houses, houses that Isham had actually seen in Rhode Island long before I was born. The text was straightforward and simple to understand. Fully half of the book had drawings of houses, their framing and layout, pages and pages of captivating information that touched every nerve in my body. I immediately checked it out of the library.

Every night after my children were asleep, I took the book to bed to read. I learned about 17th century construction, chimneys, foundations, framing and joinery details, their shape and size, how they related to each other and all the different names the parts were given. But what fascinated me the most was the way Isham used drawings to illustrate the changes a house goes through.

On one page he would draw a house the way it looked when he'd found it.

On the next page, he'd drawn its floor plan, but instead of all the lines being the same, some were fine and others heavy. In the space inside the fine lines he had written *additions*, and inside the heavy lines he'd written *original*.

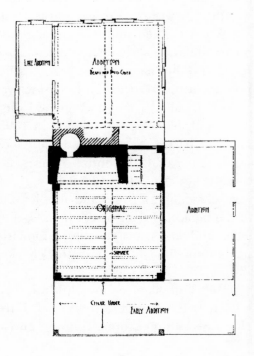

Fascinating but hard to visualize—until the next page.

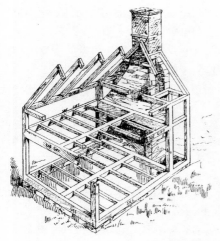

Using an eraser as an archaeologist uses a trowel, he had removed the layers of additions and then had reconstructed the original frame.

It had never occurred to me that a complete 17th century building could be buried inside what had looked to be, in the first drawing, a 19th or even 20th century house.

And then, on the following page, I looked at the sketch he'd drawn of the house as it would have looked to a passer-

by in the 17th century. I felt an archaeological calling, as if Isham had given me a trowel and said, "Now it's your turn to find and record our architectural past."

* * *

I had barely surfaced from under Isham's book when a chance was presented. A friend called to tell me about an old house slated to be burned. "It's owned by a Bill Tucker," she said, "so you better call him before taking a look."

When Bill Tucker didn't answer his phone, I figured what the heck, I'd go anyway, despite the *No Trespassing* sign, which, my friend had warned me, was posted at the entrance.

The house, on Division Road in West Greenwich, Rhode Island, was at the end of a short driveway, but far enough in to be hidden from the road. It looked as fragile as a gingerbread house that had been left out in the rain. Only a few scabs of crusty shingles were left on its front, the windows were black holes, and the bricks from the chimney lay on the roof in fragments. But there was something about its shape that looked ancient, and I couldn't help wondering if it harbored a 17th century frame. Anyway, at this point, I was so spellbound by what I had learned in Isham's book that I was convinced half of the houses I passed on the highway had a 17th century frames hidden inside.

The door, hanging by one hinge, was slightly ajar. When I tried to nudge it open, it sighed, then fell into my arms with a death rattle. I gently laid it on the ground and pointed my flashlight through the opening. The inside looked like a cave. It reeked of fungi, and most of the floor boards had rotted and fallen into the cellar—a murky pit feeding on the remains of the house. A few joists were still in place, but they looked as unpredictable as the rungs of an old wooden ladder. The only thing that looked safe enough to walk on was the huge beam in the middle that the joists had been attached to.

Tiptoeing my way down the length of the beam, I reached the fireplace hearth on the opposite side of the room. The finished woodwork and most of the plaster had rotted away, but the hearth was safe and an excellent vantage point to try out Isham's kind of reverse vision. The house wasn't in Isham's book, but I could imagine him being there, and I scratched my head trying to remember specific details he might have drawn that would indicate the 17th century. Each corner of the room did have a massive post, but that wasn't unusual. I had read that corner posts were in use as late as the early 19th century. But when I saw the huge beam that spanned the center of the ceiling, it was as if lightening had struck. This was a summer beam—exactly the kind of beam that appeared in Isham's drawings of 17th century frames. Summer beam had seemed like a weird name for a beam until I'd learned that the name was derived from the Norman French word 'sommier,' which in turn had come from the low Latin word 'sagmarius,' which meant packhorse. And now, looking at the beam, I could see exactly why. The summer beam was carrying all the floor joists.

But the summer beam was all I could identify or maybe all I knew how to recognize. And, as Isham had written, finding an ancient beam doesn't necessarily mean it is original to the house. It could have been re-used. It didn't matter. In either case it was definitely a beam that held the joists, and I still had the rest of the house to explore.

With my back to the wall I slithered by the fireplace, jumped across the cellar chasm, and grabbed on to the doorway that led to the next room. That room was strewn with pots and pans, broken furniture, soggy bits of bedding and clothing, along with the reds, blues and yellows of plastic toys. Who had lived here? Had they just walked out, closed the door, leaving everything behind—or was there perhaps a dead body under the mountain of clutter? Although it might be an ideal kind of house to study, I felt as though the 20th century had rudely interrupted my 17th century discoveries. I turned and left as fast as I could.

* * *

On the way home, I sensed there was something about the framing in the house that I had looked at but not seen.

My heart skipped a beat. Of course, how could I have missed it? Early framing methods have a summer beam under the first floor, and the beam I had walked across was, in fact, the first floor summer. Both these summers on the first and second floor were such an important part of early construction that it seemed doubtful that they were re-used. I had to go back.

*   *   *

Isham had nourished my interest in old houses, but now with a real house to study I wanted to find somebody who could answer specific questions. The only person I could think of was Antoinette Downing. I had never met her, but I had heard she was an architectural historian and had been a student of Isham's when he taught architecture at Brown University. What better person—and with luck she might be interested in seeing the house. I decided to call her.

I must have said something right because when I described the house she immediately agreed to meet at the site, and we made a date for two weeks later. I was delighted until I remembered I'd never obtained permission to be in the house and I certainly couldn't assume that Mrs. Downing wanted to be a trespasser. This time, trespassing was beyond the excuse of using a book with pictures of old houses. There was no way around it; I had to get in touch with Bill Tucker, the owner. When he finally answered his phone, I told him immediately that I'd been to the house. I think he thought I was a real estate agent as he quickly explained that the house was condemned, was going to be burned, and the land would be for sale. He was surprised when I said I was only interested in the house and was calling to ask permission to show it to an architectural historian.

"I can't imagine why," he said. "There's nothing special about it, but sure. Just don't go inside, it's too dangerous."

Relieved to have that out of the way, I walked around with a swagger, counting the days and savoring the moment when I would learn from a woman who had actually studied under Norman Isham. We planned to meet at a certain spot on the highway and from there I would lead her to the house. The day arrived. My skin tingled as I waited beside the road, nervously watching my rear view mirror, worrying she might have forgotten. Finally a car pulled up, followed by another, and still another—all filled with ladies. Bewildered, I got out of my car.

A woman, dressed in a gabardine coat in shades of muddy brown, Dr. Scholls' pumps and rolled stockings, got out of her car. She didn't smile, just nodded, then introduced herself as Antoinette Downing. I had expected to meet a vibrant and exciting woman, but her face was emotionless and her handshake cold. I asked her who were all the women.

"They are members of the Providence Preservation Society," she said," and today I'm giving them a guided tour of some restored houses."

Shocked, I tried to tell her that this was not a restored house, but she waved me aside, got back in the car and announced, "We'll follow you."

So that's what this was all about—a field trip. I was stunned. What had I said during the phone call? Had I failed to give the proper description; old and dirty and very rotten? Leading them up the driveway, I wondered how to handle this situation and, Oh God, all those ladies. There definitely would be no tea and cucumber sandwiches at this house.

After we parked, I tried again to explain to Mrs. Downing that this house was dangerous, that there was no way these women could go in, but she was too occupied trying to organizing them, as they sprang out of the cars like birds flushed from a meadow, flapping and chirping—an ambush of mink and leopard coats, stockings and high heels, anxiously awaiting a guided tour. I felt betrayed. I wanted Mrs. Downing all to myself, not lots of chattering people interrupting the quiet death of this house. I'd already heard somebody say, "What an atrocious place."

Where was the dead body when I needed it?

On the other hand, these women were members of the Providence Preservation Society and they wouldn't be here if they weren't interested. This was no time to be snobbish.

I didn't think that anyone would want to go into the house, but as they gathered at the doorway, a petite lady, dressed all in red like a lipstick out of a tube, asked me what was safe to walk on. When I pointed to the beam down the center of the room, she shrugged her shoulders and gathered her coat above her knees. But when she stretched her patent leathered foot across the threshold to reach the beam, her dress was too tight and she lost her balance. She screamed, and just in time was pulled back to safety with only her hat falling into the cellar.

Another lady, tall and thin, dressed in tweed pants and a black jacket, her hair pulled back in a bun, stepped on the threshold. As she looked around, she spied some wallpaper on the opposite side of the room and gasped, "Oh, for my collection!" In her alligator pumps, she brazenly pirouetted across the rotted joists to get to the wallpaper. When she arrived and realized what she had done, she uttered a piercing cry, then clawed at the wall as if she thought she could climb to safety. Luckily there was a window nearby, and with the help of her friends she was pulled out of danger. The rest of the women no longer had a desire to go beyond the threshold.

I'd been thinking what a curious bunch, but as I listened to them talking about the house to Mrs. Downing, I heard their comments: "how shocking; what an eye opener; I didn't think this kind of thing could happen." I realized they had never seen a house dying and were sincerely shaken.

Although I had hardly said more than two words to Antoinette Downing and had learned nothing new about early house construction, I was beginning to appreciate her role as a teacher/preservationist. She had never intended for the house to serve tea and cucumber sandwiches, only to emphasize the frailty of our architectural past. And by showing them this house, she did do that.

I returned the next day—alone.

I could have measured the house, but I didn't know how yet.

I could have saved its frame, but I didn't know yet there was a way to do that.

Instead I took three rolls of photographs.

A week later all that was left were its ashes.

Myra

Searching for old houses was more exciting for my children than baseball, dressing up dolls, or playing with the next-door neighbors. They were fascinated by the adventure, what they could find—marbles, coins, wooden toys, and with the woodwork I brought home. But the adults in my family were not fascinated. My husband was wondering who he had married. My father could see only as far as the scratches on the new station wagon. My sister called it my "silly phase," and I think, if my mother had been alive, she would have agreed with them all.

I couldn't blame them. When they looked in the barn, all they could see were piles of wood. The musty smell and peeling paint made the antique woodwork seem as shabby as a bunch of homeless people crowded in a shelter. But despite what my family thought, I knew in my bones that the material I had collected was special. I wondered, if I sold a few pieces, would my family appreciate that my collection had value?

I hated the thought of parting with anything, but I did have plenty of doors—forty in fact, stacked ten deep against a wall. Whenever I wanted to look through a stack, I had to lean each door, one on top of the next, against my shoulder. This was as risky as trying to hold back a herd of buffalo and probably a good excuse to part with a few.

I had two-paneled doors, each panel a single board averaging twenty inches in width. Some had never been painted, and some had their original hardware.

I had board-and-batten doors, a type used from the 17th century onward. These were my favorites—two wide boards joined with a decorative molding and held together with two battens across the back.

And I had many four-panel doors—doors that were popular throughout the 18th century, and a style of door, more times than not, I found in the ruins of old houses.

Anyway, I convinced myself, a door was meant to hang in a house—not hang out in a barn. But how to market them? They definitely deserved something better than a yard sale. The classified section in antiques magazines never mentioned house parts for sale, and if I advertised in the local paper my husband would claim I was planning to open a junkyard.

Feeling as though I was the only one in the world who cared, I was surprised when I received a call from a woman who lived in Norwich, Connecticut. Her name was Myra Linton, and she was barely beyond introducing herself when she told me that she collected parts from old houses. I couldn't believe what I was hearing. It had never occurred to me that there was somebody out there doing the same thing I was. I don't remember how she discovered me. It didn't matter; we were just delighted to find each other. We agreed that talking on the phone wasn't enough, and made plans to meet the following week at a house she was dismantling in the Connecticut town of Ledyard.

Dismantling a house piece by piece means bloody knuckles, plaster dust up your nose, and spider webs clinging to your eyelashes and hair. I was stunned when I arrived and found a seventy-year-old woman taking apart the house in a dress, stockings and heels. My old house costume was jeans, boots, an old shirt, and I always looked filthy. If it wasn't for the tool belt around her waist, I would have sworn she was on her way to a garden party.

She shook my hand, smiled, and said, "You didn't expect to see an old woman did you?"

"Mrs. Linton," I said, "I'm so happy to find you. I was thinking I was the only crazy person."

She laughed, "No," she said, "you should hear my family. They think at my age it's shameful to be running around the countryside filling my Cadillac with floor boards and paneling from old houses." She smiled and her rosy, plump face creased into folds.

"But isn't it exciting. Look at this marvelous 1710 house, and look at you, you're still so young and with plenty of time to prevent houses like this from being demolished."

She picked up her hammer. "Don't just stand and stare, and for heavens sakes call me Myra," she said. "Now come along, I want to show you this house, the beautiful paneling I'm removing, and hear all about what you are doing."

But, as we toured the house—a two story, center chimney house with a room on either side of the chimney and a series of rooms across the back—Myra did all the chatting.

"I haven't always taken houses apart," she said.

She explained that for thirty years she had been an antique furniture dealer. Then in the 50s, realizing that many of Connecticut's old houses were being replaced by housing developments and shopping malls, she decided that she could at least try to save their interiors.

"At first people thought I was crazy. Now collecting and selling antique woodwork is my profession," she said, then paused to catch her breath.

"But you know," she said, clapping her hands, "if I hadn't been an antique dealer first, I never would have known that certain details on furniture are often the same as those on the interior woodwork in houses. Of course that makes perfect sense. The cabinetmakers in the early 1700s also made the interior woodwork for houses. But the thrilling part was discovering that some cabinetmakers signed their name on the furniture they built."

Myra was so excited that her hair, piled on top of her head like frothy egg whites, was shaking loose.

"And because of those signatures," she said as she gathered up the escaping strands, "I have learned how to recognize each cabinetmaker's techniques. Little things, like the way a Tudor rose was carved or a molding shaped. Now, when I find these same characteristics on the woodwork in a house, I actually know who the cabinetmaker was." Her eyes sparkled.

"It makes all the in-between years drop away, and I feel as if the cabinetmaker is right in the room beside me." Embarrassed, she frantically waved the air to erase what she had admitted.

"Anyway that doesn't matter," she said, and abruptly plunked herself down on a sawhorse. But it mattered to me. I knew exactly what she felt. I was fascinated by what she was telling me, and so glad to be there that I wanted to hug her.

I told her that I knew little about Connecticut architecture, and after reading Norman Isham's *Early Rhode Island Houses*, I had assumed that early architecture, in both colonies, would be the same. That was until I read Isham's second book, *Early Connecticut Houses*, and learned that the houses weren't the same at all.

Rhode Island Stone-ender

Connecticut

Most of the early Rhode Island houses had their chimneys at the end of the house while in Connecticut the chimneys were built in the center. I had also noticed that many of Isham's drawings of two story Connecticut houses had the second story jutting out over the first—a feature, as far as I knew, rarely found in Rhode Island.

When I asked Myra why they were different, she explained that in the 17th century many of the Connecticut settlers had come from the East of England, and it was natural that they brought with them the building traditions peculiar to the area where they had lived.

"But what about Rhode Island?" I asked. "The amount of work and time it must have taken to build those huge stone ends is staggering. Especially when you think that until the house was finished there wasn't any other shelter."

"I know what you mean," Myra said, "but again the design was determined by the area the builders came from." She described how the Rhode Island stone-enders can be traced back to the West of England and Wales, where it was traditional to build a massive stone chimney on the outside end of the house.

The differences were making sense. But what I found even more interesting was listening to Myra explain how certain details, such as the way the top of a chimney was finished, the location of windows and doorways, or the pitch of a roof were like hallmarks.

"These details," she said, " can actually reveal the village in England or Wales where the carpenter came from. She beamed, "It's like house geography, isn't it?"

"However," she continued, "by the early 1700s these 'old world' hallmarks were disappearing."

The reason, she explained, was that the next generation of carpenters had discovered the need to adapt their structures to colder weather and local building materials. "Then houses in all the colonies started to take on a decided character unique to New England."

I nodded. That makes sense, I thought. I had read that by the early 1700s Rhode Islanders had started building center chimney houses. It was easy to imagine the need to have the chimney in the center of the house after experiencing the cold of a New England winter. A chimney built in the center of a house meant a family would benefit from the heat of the entire stack, not just the heat from the fireplace.

"But, it wasn't only the structure that was different," Myra said. "It was also the interior details. Come on, I'll show you." She reached for my hand, kicked the plaster and lath aside, and led me into the next room.

"In the 1700s," she said, "it was common throughout the colonies to decorate the fireplace wall in a composition of raised panels." She pointed to the wall. I caught my breath. It was magnificent and different from anything I had seen in Rhode Island. Flanking each side of the fireplace opening was a fluted pilaster with a Tudor rose carved into its top.

The area above and on either side of the fireplace had raised panels. The top row of panels shaped like a tombstone was especially beautiful.

The wall had never been painted and now mellowed by years of fireplace smoke, it had turned a rich reddish brown.

As I looked at the rest of the room, I could see that the casing on the summer beam was different. Instead of having a beaded edge on the soffit—or bottom board of its beam casing as in Rhode Island—the soffit was made up of a series of raised panels.

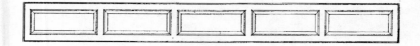

"This is amazing," I said. "It's as if there was some kind of an invisible fence at the border that kept these details from roaming."

Myra smiled, "In a way there was, but it was more to do with politics and wealth."

She explained that during the late 1600s Rhode Island was busy fighting for religious independence and therefore was a poor colony. In Connecticut the settlers were not only politically organized, but also wealthy. They could afford to pay for sophisticated interior finishes, which, in turn, gave the cabinetmakers an opportunity to show off their skills.

"That doesn't mean there aren't contradictions. For instance, look at this," Myra said, pointing to the molding around the window. "That is a typical Rhode Island molding that managed to make its way into Connecticut. And, on the other hand, don't be surprised if you find some Connecticut details in Rhode Island."

This was fascinating and I had to smile as I imagined a Connecticut cabinetmaker—with the plane he used to make a molding stuck in his back pocket—innocently crossing over the border into Rhode Island to help a friend make moldings for his house; a simple action that three hundred years later can still tease the imagination of architectural historians. And tease it has. More than forty years after I met Myra, scholars continue to perform exhaustive studies on the structural and stylistic characteristics of New England's earliest domestic architecture.

Myra opened her thermos, poured tea into two enamel cups, and handed me one. As we leaned on the edge of a windowsill, I asked her how she was able to find knowledgeable people to help dismantle a house.

"I've been lucky," she said. Then she told me about a man who was taking down an old house. Because he had wanted only the beams, he had called her to see if she wanted to buy the interior woodwork.

"When I went to look at the house," she said, "I was so impressed by how carefully he was taking it apart that ever since he and his helpers are the only people I hire."

Myra poured more tea into my mug, broke apart a brownie, and gave me a piece.

"I know this house would have been crushed by a bulldozer if you hadn't come along to save what you could," I said. "But I can't help wondering if the rooms will feel like foster children when they are separated from each other."

"Most of the rooms I rescue," she replied, "go to Henry Dupont's museum at Wintherthur. Not only is their history preserved, but there they are appreciated by the general public."

That made me feel better, and I asked her what was the best way to sell some 17th and 18th century doors.

"To me of course!" Myra said, and suddenly I was in the business.

"Wonderful," I replied. "I can't wait to tell my husband. He'll be surprised to hear that somebody actually wants them."

"Don't worry about what other people think," she said. "You and I are ahead of our times. In a few more years, you'll find a lot of people realizing how important it is to save our architectural heritage."

Myra was the boost I needed. I wasn't alone. I had found somebody who spoke the same language and who made me feel proud about what I was doing. I could have stayed there indefinitely, but I had children waiting at home and a husband who would want to know why my face was glowing.

Myra walked me to my station wagon, and I grinned when I looked at the floor boards sticking out the back of her car.

"Do you always use your Cadillac to carry woodwork?" I asked.

She laughed, "Of course," she said. "It beats driving a truck."

And every few months, Myra loaded up her Cadillac and I'd load up my station wagon, and we'd meet—on the side of the highway—half way between her house and mine. When I think of it now, I have to chuckle. The places we always seemed to end up to exchange our woodwork were right on the Rhode Island and Connecticut border. Even after three hundred years, the woodwork was still roaming.

John

Selling to Myra had freed up space in the barn and I could sense my husband's relief. But empty space can be dangerous, as now I had room enough to store a whole house. Even worse, I actually knew of one: a 1729 house that was slated for demolition. The University of Rhode Island owned the house, wanted to get rid of it, and told me I could have it for the taking. But taking a house apart—from the rafters down to the sills—meant special equipment and know-how, neither of which I had.

The idea refused to leave me alone, so I asked some local contractors if they could help. But the answers were usually, "Lady, get yourself a wrecking ball." Finally somebody told me about John Northup, a blacksmith, a carpenter, a collector of old things, and a man, they thought, who probably had even dismantled a few houses. But, they warned, "He's an independent Yankee, and crusty as they come."

John lived on Lafayette Road near Wickford, Rhode Island. His place was only a twenty minute drive and whatever had been said about him I figured I had nothing to lose, although I did wonder how he'd receive me—a woman who wanted to dismantle a house.

I drove to Wickford, found Lafayette Road and the sign that pointed to his workshop, a one story shingled building weathered to a silvery gray. I got out of my car and after following a path around a pile of bricks, a clamming skiff loaded on a trailer, an old truck without any wheels, a collection of shutters, a slate sink, some ladders, and a stack of lumber, I reached the door and knocked. No answer. I knocked again harder, and from the distance came a sharp reply, "Yup?" I figured that meant come in, so I opened the door.

A film of sawdust clung to the windows and made the light so dingy that I couldn't see where the voice had come from, but as my eyes adjusted I had no doubt that this place was a junk collector's paradise. Bits and pieces of chairs and tables, parts of houses and old belt-driven machinery lay on the floor. Overhead, stored on the tie-beams, were fishing rods, strips of molding, a pair of oars, a mast from a boat, and an old wooden sled.

The clanging sound of hammering on iron came from a room at the far end. As I walked closer, the sweet aroma of linseed oil, wood shavings and pipe tobacco led me to a doorway where I saw a man bent over a forge. He didn't look up, but continued pounding on a red-hot piece of iron.

A single light bulb hung from the ceiling. Wrecking bars and blacksmith tools sat in a corner. Cigar boxes filled with nails and jars with nuts and bolts were stacked on an old wooden workbench worn smooth as leather. Chisels, mallets, saws, and wooden clamps hung on the wall, and dozens of molding planes were neatly stacked on shelves, like books in a library.

John kept pounding on the iron, and I didn't know if I should leave, stand there waiting, or sit down in one of the three bow back chairs—the only things not covered in coal dust. A spittoon and some empty beer bottles on the floor told me these were the chairs for men who gathered to swap cracker barrel stories. I decided to stay standing.

Just when I was thinking the hell with this, I'm leaving, John grabbed his back, slowly straightened up, wiped his hands on his leather apron and turned. He was a short lean man with fraying hair and a face black with soot, but when he removed his goggles, his eyes were like two green pebbles in a field of pink skin.

"What can I do for you?" he asked, his voice crusty with impatience. From what I had seen, I didn't think he had the 'wrecking ball' attitude, but still I was nervous and afraid to admit straight out that I wanted to know how to take a house apart. Instead I asked if he used the molding planes. "Yup!" he said, "I use all of them. Some were my grandfather's, some my father's, and all the rest mine."

Then he looked back at the fire in his forge, pumped the bellows and reached for his goggles. Obviously he thought I was just another spectator, so I figured what the heck and quickly announced that I was trying to find somebody who could help me dismantle an old house.

" Well," he said, "why didn't you say so? You've come to the right place. My brother and I have done lots of that," and he put down his bellows, forgetting his fire. "What sort of a house are we talking about?"

I told him it was small, only one story, in excellent condition and with a beautiful stone chimney that had the date 1739 carved in the top.

"Where is it?"

"In Kingston, behind the University of Rhode Island. In fact it belongs to them," I said. "They've been using the land to raise pigs, but now they want to do something else and they want the house out of there."

"Hum," he said, "don't know the house."

"Well," I said, "I'm not surprised. It's way down a dirt road."

I explained how I had been riding the train from Kingston to Providence and from the window I'd spotted the top of a stone chimney on the horizon. But, I told him, the train had passed by so fast that I wasn't sure if it was my imagination, so I took the train again to see if it was real. I laughed. This had to sound pretty silly, but I continued anyway. I told him I'd seen it again, but still there wasn't enough time to spot nearby landmarks in order to find it by car. "And yes, you guessed it," I said. "I took another train ride."

I could see a tiny smile of amusement twitch at his check.

"So how **did** you find it?" John asked.

"I rode the train again and this time I saw a church steeple I recognized. Using the steeple as a starting point along with my topographical map, I drove up and down the nearby roads. Suddenly there was a house with a chimney like the chimney I'd seen from the train."

"At least I think it's the same one," I said. "But I won't really know until it's down and I go back on the train and see if the chimney is gone."

For the first time, John smiled outright. He sat on a stool and pulled a tobacco pouch out of his pocket, filled his pipe, struck a match with his thumbnail, and sucked in on the flame. I was sure he was going to ask me why I wanted to save the house, but he didn't. He seemed to assume I knew what I was after and why.

"Too bad," he said, "that there aren't more people who appreciate this old stuff. Now I'll show you the stupid things people do," and he reached over to his workbench and held up a panel from a fireplace wall. "Look at this," he said. "It's a single pine board, thirty inches wide and some damn fool cut a hole for a stove pipe right through the middle. It makes me sick. Trees don't make 'em this wide any more."

He searched through some odd shaped pieces of wood lying on the bench, then picked up a round one the size of a salad plate.

"This here is a patch called a dutchman," he said. "I've made it to repair the hole." He handed it to me and pointed to the panel. I looked at him. He nodded to go ahead and I carefully set it in place. The hole became invisible. John had chosen a piece of wood that matched the grain and color of the panel; then he'd shaped the edges with such precision that I could barely detect the seams. Not only had John returned dignity to the panel, he had added a deeper level to its history.

It was easy to see that John, an artisan, a blacksmith and a finish carpenter, cared about what he was doing, and for him any thing old was worth saving. This was the person I wanted to work with, and when I asked him if he would help me take down the house, he said, "Sure. How long do we have to get it out of there?"

I told him I'd find out and get back to him. What I didn't tell him was that I needed time to prepare my husband for the arrival of a trailer with an entire house loaded on board.

Two weeks later, I returned to John's shop with the letter I'd received from the university. "This is as good a time as any to get started," he declared after reading the letter. They had given us two months to remove the house with only two stipulations: no debris left behind and all work was to be at our own risk. Tucked into the bottom of the envelope was the key to the front door.

John still hadn't seen the house, and when I reminded him, he replied that he didn't need to. "You've explained it well enough," he said.

We worked out a deal and then agreed that the Monday of the following week would be a good time to start.

*   *   *

I woke on Monday to a brilliant day. Excited, I jumped out of bed, got breakfast for all five kids, sent them off to school, then called the baby sitter to make sure she'd remember to be in the house when they came home. I didn't want to miss a moment of taking apart this house and I had no idea what time John would call it a day. Checking first to make sure my flashlight, hammer and wrecking bars were still in my car, I took off for the site, arriving just as John appeared driving a faded red truck and pulling a trailer that had a ladder and three long poles strapped to its bed. I didn't know why he needed poles, but figured I'd find out soon enough.

John rolled down his window. "Mornin," he said. "I've brought along my brother Jim and my son Ray to help." Then he 'backed and filled' until he was satisfied that the truck and trailer were parked in a good place for loading. "That should do it," he announced, and they got out of the truck.

John's brother was broader in the shoulders and half a head taller than John while Ray was a gangly, acne faced, sixteen year old. But when I looked quickly, it was hard to tell the three apart because they all wore bib overalls and blue work shirts.

I watched John as he looked around. When he didn't say anything, my excitement faded. I remembered how he'd said I'd explained the house well enough, but now that he was seeing it with his own eyes, I wondered. The barn had fallen into its foundation, a chicken house was buckling, rusty fencing lay crumpled on the ground, the air was still soaked with the smell of pigs, and the landscape looked like a gravel pit. The only thing still standing was the house. Foxtails of dust nipped at my legs as I nervously waited for John's comment.

"Yup," he finally said, "You can tell this place has history," and he looked at Jim. "You ever been up here?"

"Nope," Jim replied. "We should have though—it's practically in our backyard."

"Well, I guess Anne one-upped us. She tends to moonlight while riding on trains," John said, and winked at Jim.

To discourage vandals, the university had boarded the windows with plywood and padlocked the door. I turned my key in the lock and opened the door into an entry hall no larger than a closet. Opposite the door, built against the chimney wall, was the stairway to the attic. As we squeezed in, a breeze rustled some loose papers lying on a step, and that's when I remembered that the last time I'd been here I'd seen other loose papers and some empty beer cans in the attic. I mentioned this to John and told him that someone had ripped the plywood off a back window and gotten into the house. But, I assured him, I hadn't found any damage, only cans and food wrappings.

As John pushed by me and up the attic stairs, I wondered if he thought somebody could still be up there or if he was simply in a hurry to see the house. I was about to follow, but a moment later he was on his way down.

His only comment, "That's a good open space. It'll make it easy to work on the roof from the inside. Let's see the rest of the house."

John, I could see, was a man of action, and I had the feeling I'd better stay close to him if I was going to learn how to dismantle a house. But first, before we went any further, I wanted to show him what I'd found behind the alcove under the stairs. The space had been walled over and fitted with a small door. The first time I opened the door, I had expected to find a storage place, the kind that old boots, mittens and baseball bats tumble out of. Instead I found a passage that led to the innards of the chimney.

I opened the door and clicked on my flashlight. With John following, we crept under the stairs and into the heart of the chimney—a hollow chamber with a sandy floor and a dizzying smell of wood tar. Poking into the space like huge fists were the reverse sides of two fireplaces. Bulging out of the back of one was the oval shape of a bake oven. It was constructed with bricks and covered with white plaster and looked just like an igloo. Spiraling upwards from the fireboxes were the chimney flues—sultry, curving shapes that came together over our heads to form an arch. As I traced the shapes with the beam of my flashlight, the mortar—a mixture of clay and crushed shells—flickered like phosphorus.

"You've discovered the inner workings of the chimney," John said, "but don't forget it's the kind of place for somebody to hide. You gotta be careful in these old houses. Came on somebody once in a closet. Scared the hell out of me."

Other than the entry hall and attic, the house had only two rooms, one to the left of the entrance and one across the back. The walls and ceilings were plastered throughout, but the framing timbers—the summer beam, corner posts and girts—had been left exposed. There was no fancy woodwork or paneling. The doors were two vertical boards held together by three battens and the fireplace mantles were a simple board with a shelf. The house's charm was the proportions of the room, the exposed frame and the stone fireplaces.

"These fireplaces are typical for here in South County," John said. He pointed to the stone lintel that spanned the opening and the stone slabs that lined the fireplace cheeks, explaining that in the northern parts of Rhode Island the lintel would be oak and the cheeks made with bricks or a bunch of small stones instead of a solid stone slab. "Makes good sense," he said. "Slabs don't crumble from the heat near as fast as small stones. Don't find stonework like this anywhere else in the state."

I followed John as he investigated the rest of the house and watched as he tapped the beams, listening for hollow sounds, and probed the wood looking for rot.

"I'm sure we'll find some rot in the sills, goes without saying," he said, while assuring me that the posts looked good and that he hadn't found any signs of termites or carpenter ants. "Up high on a hill like this makes for good clean air and those critters don't like that," he said, then jumped on the floor to prove how solid it was. All of this sounded great to me, but when he said that it was definitely worth saving, that's when I felt as though he'd blessed the house. "Should be an easy four days to get it out'a here," he said.

I didn't see how we could take the frame apart in four days. It was buried behind all kinds of stuff—roof boards, wall boards, shingles, windows, doors—and on the inside, window trim, door trim, a stairway, flooring, and what seemed like miles and miles of lath and plaster. Even the air in the rooms felt stuffed with the past. It looked like a humongous job and four days didn't seem like enough. John must have seen the doubt in my face.

"We have it easy," he said. "All the cutting and fitting was done before the house was raised. All we have to do is strip her."

John explained that the first parts to go would be the plaster and lath, the 'lipstick and rouge' he called it. Getting rid of that would be my job while they were up in the attic removing the roof boards. Then he told Ray and Jim to get the tools, go to the attic and get started. "I'll meet you boys up there," John said, "as soon as I get Anne here started on the plaster."

I hated to be called Anne. I thought of myself as Pete. I had told him that when I'd first met him. Maybe he'd forgotten or maybe he considered taking apart a house man's work and I'd have to prove myself capable before being addressed with a man's name.

"You know how to get the plaster and lath off?" he asked.

"Of course!" I told him, and waved my wrecking bar to show him I even had my own tool.

He muttered something—it sounded like "women!"—then got down on his knees to probe the floor boards.

I was about to ask if he was looking for a secret compartment when he told me he was looking for a board to pull up to get access to the cellar. I didn't say anything, but I wondered why he needed to make a hole to the cellar when the cellar stairs were right outside the back door. Fortunately I kept my mouth shut because it soon became obvious that the hole to the cellar was the quick way to get rid of the plaster and lath.

"Gotta keep this place cleaned up," he said, "or we'll be tripping all over ourselves and somebody will get hurt."

Then he told me to push the stuff I'd be knocking off the walls through the hole into the cellar—"But don't fall in yourself," he said—and disappeared up to the attic.

Using my bar, I bashed at the plaster, ducking as it fell in huge satisfying sheets. But the noise I was making was nowhere near as horrendous as the banging coming from the attic. Thinking the whole house might come down on my head, I decided to see what the three of them were up to.

Thick brown dust met me at the top of the stairs. It filled the attic, and each time Ray, John or Jim swung at the roof with a sledgehammer the dust swirled about in a rage.

"Why are you hitting the roof like that? The whole house is shaking," I yelled, choking on the dust I'd inhaled. John put down his sledgehammer, pulled a bandanna out of his pocket, swiped his face, blew his nose and told me not to worry. "Nothing's getting hurt," he said, and explained that they were only freeing the roof boards from the rafters.

"Can't reuse these roof boards, they're plain tired out— too many nail holes from repeated shingling." He convinced me that if the boards were worth saving he and his crew would be de-shingling the roof and removing each board from the outside.

"Go on back to your plaster," he said. "It won't be long now and we'll show you our trick for stripping no-good boards like these off the rafters."

I was glad to go. At least downstairs the dust from the plaster was white. Finally the banging stopped and John yelled down, "We're ready. You can go outside and watch but don't stand too close."

Except for a few new lumps, the roof didn't look any different than it had when I'd arrived. I couldn't see the men, but I could hear them shouting from inside the attic.

"Give it a nudge"—"Get your bar in here"—"Look out that's my finger"—"Damn that board is still nailed," and then—"Everyone ready? One, two, three, push."

Suddenly the peak of the roof rose up, hung suspended for a second, then flipped over.

"Once more," John hollered, and more of the roof came up and flipped over again.

But this time—helped by weight, gravity and a bit more nudging—it didn't stop. I held my breath as it somersaulted down, rolling itself up like a rug and plunging to the ground in a heap.

"Fantastic," I shrieked.

John grinned down at me. "Now for the other side," he said.

With the roof off, the rafters came alive. Each timber, like the topmast on a whaling ship, was tapered from the peak to the foot, and the sun, reflecting off the surface, made the chip marks from the shaping adze look like rippling waves. My God, I thought, compared to these, our 20th century rafters are nothing but toothpicks.

" John," I said, "they're magnificent."

"They're as sweet as they come," he said, "and I can see by the grain they're chestnut, a tree that don't grow in these parts anymore. Blight killed 'em a hundred years ago."

John handed a rope to Jim. "Times a'wasting," he said, "gotta get these rafters down." Jim got on the ladder, knotted a rope around the peak of a set of rafters, and threw the other end to Ray, who wrapped it around his arm.

"These are heavy suckers," John said, and then told me to help Ray hang on to the rope. I don't think Ray needed or wanted my help, but at least it was the first time I'd been included in the actual dismantling. Undoubtedly a test.

Ray and I hung onto the rope while John and Jim loosened

the temporary bracing and we slowly lowered the first set of rafters onto the attic floor. John knocked out the peg at the peak, then the pegs that held the collar tie. "The beam that keeps them from spreading," he said. As the pieces came apart, Ray and I dragged them to the side of the building and lowered them to the ground.

"Lucky this isn't a two story house," John said, "or we'd be using a crane to lift them off. When this wood gets old it gets heavy as lead, petrified I guess you might say. Can hardly nail into it."

He knocked out a peg and tossed it to me.

"The old timers call them tree pins," he told me. "They're oak. As strong as iron and the only things used to hold an old house together."

The peg was about four inches long—one end as fat as a cigar, the other tapering to a point.

"But how come it's crooked?" I asked.

"That happened when the house was new and still settling." John explained how the pegs had to be green wood in order to be flexible enough to twist with the house as it settled into a comfortable position. "Most of them will be crooked like that," he said. "Some so crooked we'll have to drill 'em out."

I thought about the carpenters who had built this house and how their intuitive understanding of organic elements had kept it standing for so many years.

*   *   *

I definitely had gotten behind on the plaster removal, and John scolded me, but I told him it was his fault for showing me so many fascinating things.

"How did you learn all this stuff?" I asked.

"By doing," he said. "Now let's get a hustle on or we'll never get this house out'a here." He told Ray to help me while he and his brother de-shingled the walls.

Ray and I finished pulling the lath and plaster off the ceiling, and when the dust had settled I was delighted to see that the joists had been hand planed to a smooth surface. I knew that if someone had bothered to hand plane each one, the joists were intended to be seen. This meant that the plastered ceiling was a later application. I yelled at John to come see. He scratched his head. "You know," he said, "this confirms my feelings that the construction of this house is earlier than the 1739 date on the chimney. But, if that date's right, this has got to be back-county work."

"What's that mean, 'back-country work'? It sounds like an insult."

"Nope," John said. "It's just that 1739 is late for this type of construction." He told me that by that time the joists were seldom left exposed, except by the carpenters who lived way out in the country, carpenters who were not yet aware that the folks in town were now casing the timbers and purposely hiding the joists under plaster.

"You mean they were modernizing as early as that?" I asked.

"I guess you'd call it that, but I think they were simply cutting back on labor costs: takes a lot of time to smooth out these timbers. But, by the look of these hand split laths, whoever owned this house must have made a trip to town soon after the house was built, seen what was happening, come home, split out the laths, nailed them on the joists and plastered up the ceiling. Goes to show you how dates can be misleading—dates don't mean too much to me unless I've forgotten my wife's birthday."

By the end of the day, the plaster, flooring, shingles, doors, and window frames had been removed. The only things still attached to the frame were the outside walls—wide, vertical planks, butted together and pegged to the plate and sill. John explained that like studs, the planks were the upright supports for the house. "But they do more than that," he said, and he pointed to the planks to show me that they were also used as the surface for nailing shingles on one side and plaster and lath on the other side. "Makes a lot'a sense," he said. "Carpenters back then knew how to keep a house simple but strong."

When I arrived home that night, I was covered with plaster dust and I must have looked like a ghost. My children shrieked when they saw me. "E-e-e-e," I shrieked back, and I sat down to explain what I had been doing.

"This time, instead of taking apart some of a house," I said, "I'm taking apart a whole house and when I get through I'll bring it home to you." Then I told them about John's trailer and big dump truck and how he'd said he'd be able to bring the whole house to us in one load. They cocked their heads. They were just as disbelieving as I was. Except, now that the roof boards and the shingles were off and the plaster knocked down, I was able to see how uncomplicated a frame is. Even though it is the heart of a structure, it consists of only twenty or so major pieces. Taken apart, all its pieces, including the sheathing boards, flooring and floor joists, just might make it home to us in one load.

The next morning John announced that we couldn't do anything more until we cleaned up. There were shingles and roof boards on the ground and, because the cellar was now full, a pile of plaster and lath in the house. It took most of the morning to drag the rubble to the nearby barn foundation and burn it. By noon I was thinking that the biggest amount of time taking down a house was cleaning up after ourselves— that was until we closed our lunch boxes and John assigned me another endless job—de-nailing the boards. "Gotta take every nail out," John said. Not only would they scratch things up, he explained, but they'd also prevent the load from lying neat and flat on the truck. I hated this job. The nail heads were set so deep into the boards that I couldn't pull them out with the claw on my hammer. Instead they had to be banged out from their opposite end, and because they were wrought-iron instead of steel, it wasn't easy. Each time I'd hit one with the hammer, it would roll up like a caterpillar—and it didn't matter how many times I unrolled them, they'd roll up again the next time. John laughed when he noticed me struggling to unroll a nail.

"That's why wrought-iron nails are so good for clenching," he said. "You can make them bend over and back into the wood. Now give me the hammer and I'll show you a trick."

He gave the head of the nail a whack, then turned the board over and hit its opposite end. The nail shot out as straight as a pencil.

"Problem is the nail tends to get rusted in place and you gotta hit it to break its grip. Here's a can to save them in. Each nail is handmade, and if I had to make 'em new it'd cost ten cents a piece."

* * *

I had blisters, three on the palm of my hand, a black and blue thumb that had gotten in the way of my hammer, and stubborn dirt under my fingernails that even mechanic's soap couldn't make disappear. A detail my husband hadn't noticed until the end of the second day of working with John. "Those are not hands of a wife," he grumbled.

"Perhaps," I said, and asked him to please come and see the house so he would understand what I was doing. But he shook his head and told me he had other things to do.

The next morning, I felt fresh, ready and anxious to learn how John would dismantle the frame—the only thing still standing. In my rush to get home to the children at the end of the previous day, I hadn't stopped to look back at what we'd accomplished and I wasn't prepared for the emotion that swept over me when I drove up to the site. The frame, with a haunting fundamental beauty, filled the sky with the outline of shelter just as it had on the day of raising. I must have looked dazed. John walked over.

"You okay?" he asked.

"Sure," I said, blinking away the sting in my eyes.

"You know," John said, "each piece of that frame was cut out of the forest, then shaped by hand. Wasn't no architects, sawmills, chain saws, skill saws, table saws, and all that electric stuff we have today—just gut knowledge of how to build shelter. Mind you, the only tools used to birth this house was an axe, an adze, a pit saw, a chisel, a smoothing plane and a mallet."

"And a keg of rum on the day of raising," I added.

"Yes," John said. "You can bet your boots a lot of rum was drunk at the end of that day." Then he picked up his hammer and yelled, "Okay, boys, let's get this frame down," and he began to drive out the pegs that had been holding it together for two hundred and fifty years.

* * *

The first timbers to come off were the plates—the long beams on the front and back of the house. They lay across the top of the posts and were the footings for the rafters. But John explained that because they were connected to the posts by a mortise and tenon they also served as clamps to hold the posts in place, and then he asked me if I knew what a mortise and tenon was. Before I had a chance to nod yes, he continued to explain

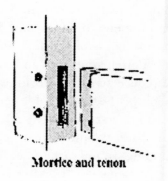

Mortise and tenon

that a tenon was like a plug cut into the end of a beam and a mortise was the socket on another beam that the tenon fitted into and then locked in place with a peg.

"All the joints in this house are like that, male and female like, if you know what I mean, but bet you didn't know that most of this frame was pegged together on the ground and then raised in sections." He pointed to the two posts and the girt—the horizontal beam that connected to the posts at ceiling height. The girt was as long as the width of the house and lots of work was expected of it. It held the posts upright, shouldered the summer beam—the center support for the joists—and was the top timber that the vertical planks were attached to. John called the units bays. This house was small so it had only three: a section, or bay, at each end and one in the middle for the chimney. The first two sections outlined a room.

So far I understood how the sections were put together—like a prefab—and how they outlined a room, but I couldn't understand how, after they'd been raised, the summer beam had been installed between. It was a huge beam that spanned the room at ceiling level. I knew that each end of the summer had a tenon and the tenon could only be fitted into the sections before they were standing upright in their final position. It looked as complicated as a Chinese puzzle.

"It's simple," John said. "You'll see. It's gonna come down the same way it was put up."

He told Ray and Jim to get the three long poles and the block and tackle from the trailer.

After they brought everything over, they made an A-frame by tying the tops of the poles together and then attaching the block and tackle to the top. When that was done, they lifted the poles up and straddled their legs over the summer beam. Jim tied a rope around the summer, hooked it to the block and tackle, and took a strain on the rope to keep the summer from falling while John and Ray removed the first wall of a section.

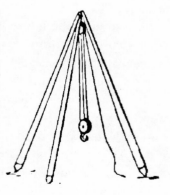

"A poor-man's crane," John said.

Yankee ingenuity, I thought.

When the first section was down, John was able to wiggle the tenon at the other end of the summer out of the second section. And when they laid it down, the summer was left suspended in air like a monolith. It was unnerving—it must have weighed a ton—and I held my breath as they fed out the rope attached to the block and tackle and slowly lowered the summer beam down—exactly in the reverse of how it had been hoisted in place so many years ago.

"Anne, get some rollers under it," John shouted when the summer was almost at floor level. Rollers, I realized, were the only way it could be moved to the truck—and as we slowly rolled it across the field I got thinking about the massive stones that people—four thousand years ago—had rolled twenty miles, from Marlborough to Salisbury, in order to build Stonehenge. My summer beam seemed just as noble.

With the summer beam removed, the last two sections came down quickly and the only timbers still in place were the sills and first floor joists. The joists lifted out easily, but the sills had been patched so many times that they weren't worth saving, so we dragged them to the burn pile.

"Just because we un-raised a house doesn't mean we can't celebrate," John said. "I don't have any rum but I have plenty of beer. Son, you know where they are, bring 'em over."

We toasted the house, the carpenters who had built it and then each other, until Jim finally said, "You know, we still gotta load that trailer." And without much enthusiasm we started. We were halfway done when John looked at me and said, "You know, we haven't marked anything. If you ever wanted to put this back up you'll have to match up the Roman numerals that were used to identify the pieces when the frame was first cut out," and he pointed to a mortise and tenon. "See how the mortise on this post and the tenon on that girt are both marked with a VII. That means they go together.

Every joint in this house is hand carved like that, fitted, and given its own set of Roman numerals. I nodded. "But look here," he said. "This is a different kind of mark that's been scratched into the wood," and he slowly traced his finger around a circle with a line through the middle. "It's called a scribe, but I call it the language of the house builder. Beats me what this one means but sure as hell the carpenter knew. Could be as simple as where a door would go."

I touched the mark and wondered how many other things there were to learn. It seemed that in an old house there was a sense of human hands everywhere.

* * *

"What do you want to do about the chimney and door stones?" John asked. Now that the chimney was standing alone, out in the open, I could see how perfectly each stone had been chiseled to fit with the next one.

"We can't leave them behind," I told him. John said it would take three loads to get all the stones to my place, and when unloaded it would make "one hell of a pile."

I shuddered. I hated to think what my husband would say when a pyramid emerged in our backyard.

"Look," John said, "I can use them, especially the fireplace stones and the one with the date. How about we trade a day of work and I'll take them to my place."

"Agreed," I said, "as long as I can keep the front door stone." I wanted to place it at the entrance to my garden where bare feet could flirt with its velvet surface—a surface worn smooth by generations of footsteps.

* * *

The fourth day was moving day. After the trailer and truck were packed, John secured everything with ropes. "That's it," he said.

I looked at him. "You mean this load really is the entire house that was standing four days ago?" It still seemed bewildering. There was such a small amount of material compared to the amount of shelter the house had provided, as if we had taken its lungs without the air.

"Okay, boys," John said. "Let's get going. It'll be dark soon, and we still gotta unload this at Pete's house."

And when he said "Pete," I tried not to smile. I didn't know if it was the beer or an official declaration that I was now a full-fledged member of the crew. I searched his face for a clue, but when he looked at me all he said was, "You bring up the rear and if things start to slip, blow your horn."

*   *   *

"They don't make houses like this anymore," John said as we unloaded the last piece into the barn. I looked at the stack of timbers that had been a house—a house carved out of a forest, shaped by man, lived in by generations—and now that it was lying in the barn it seemed it had circled back into itself. I certainly had no plans to put it back up. It was just that it was in such good condition and early enough that it simply seemed important to save. If nothing else, someday, somebody might want to use some of the timbers for something.

"By the way," I yelled at John, as he started to drive off, "I'm taking another train ride and if that chimney is still on the horizon I'll let you know."

Business Cards

John continued to help me, and three years later I had two more houses stored in my barn, and in my head a multitude of hands-on experiences. John had taught me how a house was put together and how to take it apart, but I still hadn't learned how **not** to hear a house cry out "save me." Either I'd have to stop listening or come up with a better solution than flat on their backs in a barn.

Fortunately, as I was dismantling my third house, a newspaper reporter got wind of what I was doing. It was 1965 and plans for the bicentennial were churning. The reporter thought saving old houses would make an interesting story. He came to the site, asked questions, and took pictures. The following Sunday, in the Home Section of our newspaper, the headline read "She Loves House Work." A pun that hit too close to home when my husband said, "Yeah! Since when?"

But despite the headline, the reporter did me a great service. He explained how a house could be dismantled and re-erected, and referred to me as an expert—changing my status from amateur into professional overnight. In no time I was getting serious inquiries from people who hadn't known that dismantling was possible. It wasn't long before I had a telephone call from a man who said, "I didn't know you could take apart a house until I read the article about what you were doing," and then explained that his 18th century family homestead was in the path of a new highway. Despite his efforts, the state refused to re-route the road. He told me he didn't have a site to move it to, but he had to do something or it would be demolished.

"Can it be dismantled and stored while I look for land?" he asked.

"Yes." I said. And I had my first client.

Pleased with myself, I ordered a thousand business cards, and when they arrived with the name *A.W. Baker Restorations* in bold blue letters, I felt as though I'd awarded myself a diploma. However, if I was going to offer a real service, the procedures John and I had been using would have to be expanded. Being able to deliver the parts and pieces of a house was one thing, but delivering it in a way that it could be reassembled was another. Without measured drawings, a set of plans, a marking system for identifying each piece, photos of construction details, a record of architectural changes, and a research of all the previous owners, it would be like delivering a book with pages missing. I explained this to John and asked him if he'd continue to help.

"Nope," he said, "sounds too professional. I like to get them down and out fast as possible. Numbering takes too much time. Easy enough to figure out what goes where when you need to."

The idea of measured drawings didn't sit well with him either.

"An old house already is what it is," he said, "and doesn't need one of them fancy architects. The only measurements you need are its length and width, so you'll know what size house you got."

John was stubborn and I knew there'd be no way to convince him that my ideas were essential.

"You'll do fine without me," he said. "Just remember how to listen. When you treat a house right, you'll hear it say 'ahh' and when you don't, surer than hell you'll hear it scream 'ouch'."

Hearing the 'ahh' and the 'ouch' was critical but not enough. I had to be sure a house would be delivered with its history intact and a guarantee it could be re-erected even if I wasn't around.

*　　*　　*

I was on my own. I had a client and my name on a thousand business cards, but I didn't have a John and I didn't have a crew. Somehow I had to find at least three people to help me.

Fortunately, the timing was right. By the mid 60s, the hippie era had reached full swing and it wasn't difficult to find young people who were searching for their roots. Peeling back the layers of a house was one way of doing that and there were plenty who were fascinated by the idea and wanted the job. I hired three. One had huge muscles—needed; one owned a truck—indispensable; one owned a ladder—useful. All three had gorgeous long beards.

My new crew was enthusiastic and anxious to start. I immediately had doubts. I wasn't worried about the physical dismantling; I could teach them that, but would they know how to hear the 'ahh' and the 'ouch'?

And then there were the additional procedures I'd promised myself were necessary: first, measure every room and every detail then transfer the figures to paper—but the only space I'd ever measured and recorded on paper was my clothes closet; second, create a system for marking each piece so whoever put the house back together would know which piece went where—but how to make that make sense? third, find the names of all the owners by searching through deeds at the town hall—but the only deed research I'd completed was on my own house and that was easy because my grandmother had all the records. Compared to my other options, taking photos was looking like a snap—aim and click.

But most important, if I was going to be a professional, was to record all the architectural changes I might find. Except I hadn't taken apart enough houses to know how to recognize re-used pieces that told about change to the house. And I didn't know that change could be as mischievous as children playing hide and seek; feather boards, shelving and paneling reused as sub-flooring or a patch in the ceiling, a girt with empty mortise pockets, a summer beam reused as a post, outside clapboards under the plaster on an inside wall, or a mark of an earlier roof line in the attic. And I didn't know that change required knowing how to look back and forth, up and down, through the first floor, the second floor, the attic, the cellar—in order to find where a piece originally belonged.

Even now, after years of experience, change continues to be mischievous. Not long ago I was asked to examine a house. It seemed perfectly normal. Anyway it looked normal, that is it looked like a one story house with a nice 17th century frame. But as I wandered through I kept thinking something didn't feel right, like walking with my shoes on the wrong feet. It wasn't until I went into the cellar and discovered that the first floor ceiling girts were now the sills that I realized the whole first floor had been cut out and the second floor was now the first. Outlandish when you think of the amount of work it must have been to make that change; remove the stairs, the fireplace, and the furniture, knock out the walls, cut away the first floor posts, and jack down the second floor without getting squashed. Perhaps the mother-in-law had threatened to move in.

And somewhat later there was a two story, center chimney house—except one half was missing, and that was very confusing as it meant that the middle of the house was now its end. I knew the other half had been there because I found a plastered wall under the shingles. Finally a neighbor told me about two brothers who had lived in the house. They didn't get along, so one lived in one half and one in the other. One day they quarreled and one of them said, "I've had enough!" and he packed up his belongings and his part of the house and moved it down the road—and that's were I had to go to find the missing piece.

But I hadn't had experiences like those when I started on my first client's house. So I decided to find out all I could about his house before taking measurements or lifting a hammer—old photographs, the names of past owners, even tales from the neighbors might help.

The neighbors' comments, however, started and ended with, "That old place? It's been around forever." But when I visited the local historical society and found an old photograph, I found my first clue to its past. The photograph was dated 1873, and since then two additions had been added, confirming my suspicion that no parts of either addition were old. What was intriguing, though, was the chimney. Its present location was different from the one in the picture. This could mean the house had gone through some major changes.

I xeroxed the photograph and headed for the town hall where I hoped to find the names of all the owners—information I planned to give to the new owner. For me, however, finding the names of the owners meant I could find their wills, and a will, I'd been told, sometimes includes a description of the house and possibly clues about changes that had been made over the years. As soon as I saw the town hall, I suspected that this wasn't going to be too easy. It wasn't just a town hall, it was an institution. Built in the 1890s, the brick edifice was large and imposing, and when I entered and walked down its marble hall my footsteps echoed off closed doors—doors advertising the tax collector, police department, highway and building department, the health and cemetery department, the dog officer, and finally the registry of deeds. I pushed that door open and was confronted by hundreds of leather-bound books stacked on shelves up to the ceiling. Oh my God, I thought, this is what three hundred years of land transactions look like, and all I had was the name of the last owner and the name of a street.

The woman in charge took my information, looked at a plat map that showed streets and building lots, wrote down some numbers on a slip of paper, handed me the paper, pointed to the top row of a shelf, and then pointed to a ladder.

Now these books are thick and heavy and all I could think, as I lifted the book and started down the ladder, was what would happen if I dropped it and all that land spilled out on the floor. I hung on tight, was ushered into a little room, and the door was closed.

I was alone with three centuries of properties stuffed in a book. As I opened the cover, a dry musty odor of time spilled out. The first page was smothered in words elegantly shaped with a quill. The ink was so old it had oxidized to the color of russet brown.

The date at the bottom of the first deed was 1672— too early, I felt. Anyway there were so many old fashioned words that I couldn't understand what land they were talking about. I decided I'd better start at the back and work forwards. I turned the book over, opened the back cover, and found the 20th century. The writing was much easier to read and I found the deed I was looking for. It was written in 1932 and described the cement posts that marked the boundaries and the abutters' names. I followed the names back and found the person who had owned the property in 1893. In theory it should have been easy, but the further back I went the more confusing the descriptions became. The street changed to a road, then to a lane. The land got larger and larger. The cement markers changed to stonewalls, then a walnut tree, a sapling and a brook that probably was now under the A&P. It got so complicated that I didn't know if I was even reading the description of the same piece of land I'd started with. Okay, I thought, I'll follow the abutters' names back. If the different abutters keep being abutters of the land I was trying to identify, then maybe I'd have something.

I started again in the 20th century, and followed the deeds backwards until I was sure it was working—that is, that the names of the people who had owned the property coincided with the names of each abutter each time the land had changed hands. Six hours later I emerged with five names of people who at one time had owned the land and the house. I picked the name of an owner who had died in 1722 and asked to see the will. "Not my department," the woman said, and she sent me down the hall with instructions to look for a door that said *Probate Records*.

With the name and date of death, it was easy to find the will I wanted. It read as follows:

"I give to my wife the use and improvements of my keeping room and bedchamber above; all the yarns hanging from the summer beam and a privilege to use the fireplace, its cooking utensils and bake oven and I give my son Caleb, a good and honest boy, the privilege of building a lean-to against the great stone chimney of my house."

It was clear, as if a print had come up in a darkroom, that the house was originally a two room, two story house with an exposed end chimney. It would be doubtful, after three hundred years, that much of the original parts of the house would still be there, but now at least I knew what to look for. Just thinking about it made my fingers tingle. I raced back to tell my crew what I'd discovered.

They'd been sweeping out the house, and as I described what I'd found and told them we could be involved with a three-hundred-year old house, their eyes bulged.

One scratched his beard and said, "You mean, a little old house is buried underneath these walls?"

Another said, "It's like it's been gift wrapped and we get to unwrap it."

The third looked around as if he was trying to x-ray the walls. Then with a look of concern he said, "We're going to have to be very careful taking this house apart."

I'd heard enough to know that I had three people I could trust, and I set them to work removing the plaster.

*   *   *

It was a big house and would take my crew a few days to knock the plaster down and shovel it out. This would give me time to start measuring the house and draft a set of plans, something my professional side had told my amateur side to do. John was right; the house already was what it was and didn't need an architect. Instead my plans would show every detail of the house: the floor boards, the trim, the doors, the windows, the baseboards, the moldings, and the frame—all drawn to scale. Once that was down on paper, I'd have a place to record my marking system so whoever re-erected the house would know where all its pieces belonged. But even more important, the plans would become its family tree. A document that would show each layer of change, and all its construction methods.

But I still had to learn how to do that. I bought a book, *Drafting Made Simple*. It told me to buy a T-square, a triangle, dividers, a scale ruler, and a big roll of paper, which I did, and then went to see an architect friend. In no time he taught me how to take the measurements, how to use the scale ruler to translate the feet into inches, and how to turn that information into lines on a piece of paper. It seemed pretty straightforward except he hadn't told me that lines of an old house refuse to conform to the rules of drafting. It was impossible to get the front and back of the house to stay parallel when the measurements were transferred to paper. And then the line for the end of the house refused to meet the line for the top of the house at a clean right angle. This meant many trips between my drawing board and the house to check and recheck the measurement that I'd already measured three times. I tried to blame it on my ruler or a defective T-square, but in fact, it was just the house, and every old house I've measured since. Like old people, old houses get twisted and bent, and the best I could do was to pick the middle point between the extremes.

When the drawings were completed, I could no longer put off figuring out a system for marking the pieces of the house. A system that would be easy for anybody to understand when the pieces were put back together.

I'd read a book about early houses that had illustrations to go with the text. The author had lettered each room in the illustrations as a way to identify the areas he was writing about. Definitely a good solution. I wrote the letters of the alphabet on separate pieces of cardboard, but as I pinned them up in each room, I realized I hadn't considered the possibility of having more rooms than letters of the alphabet. The house was big with many rooms, and by the time I got to the letter T, I was keeping my fingers crossed—probably a good idea because when I was finished, only the letters X, Y, and Z were left over.

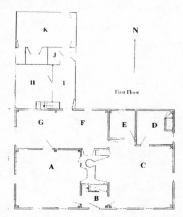

But lettering rooms also had interesting side effects. With the letters tacked up, house dismantling took on a language of its own.

"Hey, you in B, I need your help up here in P," or "I think this piece I found in S is the missing one that belongs in D," or "Watch out for N, the floor is falling in." A visitor might have thought I was running a kindergarten.

Everything was going according to plan or at least the plan I was planning for. I'd found out something about the house and its owners, taken lots of photographs, made a set of plans, and decided how the room letters could be the leading edge for my marking system.

Some rooms had as many as fifty separate pieces of wooden trim to be removed. One window alone could involve ten different pieces of wood. Then there were the baseboards, wainscoting, door trim and moldings, shelving, floor boards and doors—and I had promised myself to number every one of these pieces.

Suddenly the outlines I hated making in school made sense. I remembered that the headings had letters and the subheadings numbers. I started in room *A*. The first piece I removed was the molding. I marked it *A.1.*, and then recorded that information on its matching image I'd drawn.

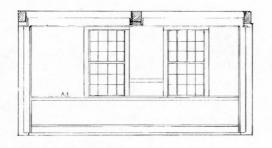

Room A.
West wall

I was pleased at how well my system was working until I removed *A. 4.* and found an earlier piece of trim under the piece I had just removed. No problem, I thought. If the first piece is *A. 4.*, then the underneath one will be *A. 4.a.* But finding a generation of pieces behind pieces puts a deep strain on the numbering system. In the case of the Mott house, which I'm saving to tell you more about later, that's exactly what happened. I removed the top tread on the stairway in *B* room. I gave it a *B.1.*, and the one I found under it, a *B.1.a.*, then entered the letters and numbers on the plans. But, under the second tread there was a third tread, and then another under that. Before I was finished, I'd found four separate treads all from the same step. The final one got a *B.1, a.,b.,c.* and the margin of the plan got lots of notes and arrows.

As hard as it was on my marking system, finding the 'extra' pieces was like reading an autobiography. These pieces were part of the story the house was telling, like finding hidden handholds of time. Even though the 'extras' probably wouldn't be used again, I wasn't about to throw away a visible link with the past.

* * *

Removing trim requires patience, not muscle. That means gentle persuasion while waiting to hear it say "ahh." A woman is ideal for this work. But it occurred to me, while standing there holding the wrecking bar under a piece of molding in a sort of time-lapse position—that one of the crew might think—because I was a woman—I was too weak to pull the molding free, and he'd try to yank the bar down. Before that happened, this was a perfect time to get the crew together and give them a lesson in how to listen to a house. They gathered around me and watched as I forced my bar under a piece of worthless picture molding, then gave a jerk. It broke with a loud crack. "That's an 'ouch'," I told them. Then I gently put my bar under another piece, gave it a little pressure and waited. When the piece finally gave a sigh, they smiled and in unison cried out "ahh." And for the rest of the day, throughout the house I could hear them singing ahh-h-h-h, up and down the scale. They'd definitely gotten the point.

The crew was fantastic. They had caught on quickly, had come up with some useful suggestions, and had actually recognized a timber that was part of the earlier house. Even though it was taking longer than I'd expected, I knew we were proceeding correctly. Despite John's reluctance about professionals, I think he would have been proud.

Satisfied with the way things were going, we swung into full gear. I'd rented a forty-foot flatbed for the beams and a trailer for storing all the interior material. This way, when the house was all dismantled, it would be easy to move to a new site.

After the flooring was removed, the only thing left to walk on was a board path laid across the joists. One of the guys in the crew, forgetting to follow the path, fell through to the cellar with a crash. A frightening sound, followed by a horrible silence, but he came up smiling and with no broken bones. I'm amazed when I think back to the 60s and 70s. Nobody who worked for me had accident insurance. It was a crutch, they said, and made one less careful. They still stepped on nails, banged their thumbs and occasionally fell through the floor, but there was a silent understanding that they alone were responsible for their actions. Today you'd say I was lucky that nobody was seriously hurt or that I wasn't sued. But until the 80s, suing others for your own mistakes simply didn't happen—at least in the business of old houses. That breed of individuals is no more. Now we all have insurance.

Next we removed the roof boards—the way John had taught me—and then the clapboards. Each clapboard was numbered, then bundled with others and placed in the trailer. Protected by layers of paint, the clapboards were in good condition. Some even had their original hand wrought nails. I didn't know if the owner would use them, but at least he'd been given the option.

After we had removed the sheathing, the only thing left to take apart was the frame. This was a big, two story, house—the posts were sixteen feet tall and the girts twenty-eight feet long—too much for the four of us to handle alone which meant hiring a crane. The beams, each strapped with 2x4s for extra protection, were lifted by a cable, one by one, and loaded on the flatbed. As I watched the first one sail over my head like a ship heading for a safe harbor, I thought I might have a romantic collapse. In fact I was thinking about crying until one of the guys in

the crew waved to the beam as it passed overhead and shouted, "The Lone Ranger rides again."

"Hi, Ho Silver," I shouted back and hugged each crew member. We'd done a hell of a good job. The house was safely down and on its way. Nothing to cry about.

ANNE W. BAKER

When I looked at the house neatly stacked on the flatbed, I felt I had fulfilled my promise to myself and the house. Not only had we saved it from being crushed by a bulldozer, but we were delivering it with measured drawings, a marking system, photos, list of owners, and as much of its architectural history as I was able to recognize.

One thing kept bothering me though—when the house was re-erected it wasn't going to be the same. Sure, all the parts were there and would be put back in their same places, but it would smell different, the plaster would be new, there would be no artifacts or layers of history to discover, the house would be too level and even the ghosts would be gone. Granted, it still had its original proportions, its original beams, trim, flooring, doors and windows, but somewhere along the line its bond with the past would be broken. That's when I started thinking about the fireplaces and how they are the focal point of a room; a place where generations had warmed their hands, baked their bread, burned evidence of love affairs, fought their wars and told their secrets. A fireplace was the soul of a house and if I could find a way to preserve its essences, it could be the anchor that would keep the past and the present together.

When I moved the next house, my fourth, I thought about numbering each fireplace brick so they could go back exactly as they had been originally, but that was crazy as the mason would either triple his price or walk off the job. Instead I packaged the bricks from each fireplace so at least when they were rebuilt it would be with their own original bricks. But that didn't work either. When it was finished, it looked like what it was—new. So I thought, why not move a fireplace intact. But how?

I talked about the idea with other people, and one day somebody told me they knew a guy named Dean Saglio, who had a machine that sprayed foam into hollows. The foam, he explained, would expand and turn rigid. This sounded interesting and might be the solution for keeping a fireplace from collapsing in on itself when lifted out of a house. I called

Dean and explained that I was trying to find a way to move old fireplaces without taking them apart.

"I've done that," he said. "Come see me and I'll show you how the stuff works. Right now I'm using the foam to insulate between the walls of a house."

He gave me the directions to the house where he was working, and when I arrived I saw a man in his thirties dressed in tattered shorts unloading a truck of sheet rock. He was shirtless and either his arm had a tattoo or was smudged with dirt. I yelled hi, and walked over. He looked up. His eyes, slanted above high cheekbones, flashed with friendliness. I told him my name was Pete and I was the person who had called about his foam machine.

"You've the one that wants to move a fireplace," he said.

I nodded my head and followed him into the house.

The machine looked like a house generator, except it had a funnel on the top and a hose coming out of the side.

"Watch," he said, then started the motor and aimed the nozzle into a barrel.

The stuff that came out of the nozzle looked like toothpaste, but as I watched, it began to squirm, then expand, and then fill the barrel with foam.

"Wait a few minutes before you touch it," he said. "The chemicals that make this stuff work are hot."

When he told me it was okay to touch, I was amazed to find it had already turned rigid.

"With this stuff," he said, "I can move a fireplace intact."

"You're hired," I told him. I didn't question it—I had nothing to lose.

* * *

We planned to try foaming a second floor fireplace, the smallest one in the house. But first the roof and then the chimney stack above the fireplace had to be removed. When the stack was down to the top of the fireplace, I called Dean.

Two days later he arrived at the site, looked at the fireplace and said, "Piece of cake."

First he removed the brick hearth, then dug tunnels under the fireplace and inserted steel rods. The rods, he told me, would hold the fireplace while he separated it from the chimney below. When he had six rods in place and the debris dug out, he shoved a sheet of plywood under the rods, then mixed up some cement, and poured it into the area.

"That's its lifting pad," he explained while attaching a steel cable to the ends of the rods. "I'll be back tomorrow when the cement has hardened."

The next day Dean arrived with his foam machine in tow. It took four people to lug it to the second floor. When it was in place, he fed chemicals into the funnel, started the engine and aimed the nozzle into the fireplace. The foam oozed out and slowly expanded. He sprayed some more until the inside was filled. When the foam had turned rigid, he boxed the outside of the fireplace with plywood and announced he was ready. I felt this was going to work. It looked so well crated that I was sure it could be shipped to China. But it still had to be lifted off.

The crane operator switched on his motor, maneuvered the boom over the house and lowered its hook. Dean picked up the other end of the cable, attached it to the lifting pad, looped it over the hook and signaled thumbs up. The fireplace rose as gently as a hot air balloon, and just as gently the crane operator lowered it

down on a flatbed. Six months later, when it was lifted into its new location, the plywood removed, the foam scraped out, and a fire lit, the soul of the house had been returned.

There was no stopping. Moving fireplaces this way became a routine—the biggest so far, a fifteen-ton mass that included two back-to-back stone fireplaces and a bake oven. And every time a fireplace was reinstalled intact, I knew that the soul of the house had been saved.

* * *

Dismantling a house only happens a couple of times a year so I couldn't always depend on the availability of the same crew. Over the years I have worked with at least thirty different people and I have yet to find anybody who worked on an old house who didn't get hooked for one reason or another. Now, years later, it tickles me when somebody touches me on the shoulder and says, "Remember me? I worked with you on the such and such house." And like old schoolmates, we'd start reminiscing about the time we took down a wall and found a gold coin wrapped inside a list of whorehouses or the time somebody found a loaded flintlock pistol stashed under a floorboard. We might remember that lady who brought us tea in a wine bottle, and the policeman who thought we were vandals and tried to put us in jail. But especially we'd talk about the house that turned out to be a genuine 1661 Rhode Island stone-ender.

* * *

By the time the bicentennial had come and gone, I had used up three boxes of business cards. Not only were people trying to save old houses, now there were people who just wanted one, even if it meant shipping it to Alaska.

Moving

Dismantling a house is one way to save it. Moving a house in one piece is another—and a much better method. The original house remains the same, its historic fabric isn't destroyed, and the cost is far less than the cost of taking a house apart and putting it back together.

The first time I moved a house in one piece, it was my own. Not my grandmother's house, where my first husband and I lived, but an old house I discovered, moved, and then moved into with my new husband. A moving experience that was set in motion on a winter morning in 1963, when my telephone rang.

"Is Pete there?" a man asked.

"That's me," I replied. "How can I help you?" He said his name was Bob Baker and asked if I was the person with antique woodwork for sale.

"I'm looking for an old mantel," he said.

I assured him that I had an extensive collection and we arranged an appointment for the following Wednesday. Innocent enough, until Wednesday at 10:00 when he knocked on my door and I opened it. First I noticed his shiny black hair that lay like a mane on his forehead, then his canvas coat with elbow patches, his leather boots and the blue wool scarf flung casually around his neck. He looked gorgeous, like an explorer who had just returned from an exotic adventure. And when he removed his pipe and grinned, his eyes—the color of green polished glass—glowed as if the tide had just washed over them. There was no need for "hello"—it was if we had always known each other, and I knew my life was about to change.

I can't remember how we got to the barn or even how I managed to sell him some woodwork. We kept discovering each other and how nicely we fit together. He, too, loved old houses, and was a collector. Because he was a marine architect, his main interest was collecting old boats, but he had some old cars, and even some old house parts. Before he left, I agreed to meet him at an old house he wanted to show me, and then of course there were boats to see and then more houses, and over the next few months our relationship became solid. I had discovered a way to be me in combination with another.

By the end of a year, my husband had agreed to a divorce. Bob and I were married and the kids went back and forth between our two houses, except our house, Bob's and mine, was a boat—a big one—eighty-three feet long. She was a real antique, built in 1908. My children loved being aboard, but by 1967, after the birth of two more children—a nose count of seven—eighty-three feet had absolutely, definitely, gotten too small.

Not wanting to get away from the water, just off it, Bob and I decided to look for a house in Westport, Massachusetts, a peninsula of land jutting into the ocean, where Bob had lived before I'd met him.

We didn't want to get involved with a real estate agent until we had looked around on our own. Warren, Rhode Island, where our boat was berthed, was only a half hour from Westport. Whenever we had a chance we'd pack a picnic, and with the two youngest, who weren't yet in school, drive over to Westport and look for houses with a *For Sale* sign in front. But the houses were either too small, too new, or smack on the edge of a road, and nothing was next to the water. Even though we weren't in a hurry, we routinely checked the real estate section of the newspaper every Sunday. And suddenly there it was: *For Sale by owner. Seventy-acre farm. Two aluminum barns. Two story house. River frontage.* Exactly the parts we wanted. At the bottom was a telephone number which I immediately called. I told the man who answered that my husband and I had seen the ad and wondered where the farm was. He gave me the address, and explained that he didn't live there as he had only recently inherited the farm from his father.

"But," he said, "you're more than welcome to take a look at the property. The address is 670 Drift Road." If we wanted to get inside the house, we could call him and he'd meet us there with the key. I thanked him, told him we might take a look, hung up, and relayed the conversation to Bob. Ten minutes later we'd left the kids with a friend and were on our way to Westport.

Luckily, for once, I didn't romanticize about what we'd find because when we arrived I saw a depressing mess.

"What's happened?" I said. "This land looks horrible, like a body that's had its skin scraped off."

"That's just about it," Bob replied. "The land has been stripped of its gravel. It happened about four years ago, around 1962, when the state decided to build a new road through the middle of Westport."

Then he explained that Westport sits on a gravel moraine and because gravel was needed as a sub base for the new road, the state had offered to buy the gravel from local farmers. The state said they would push the topsoil aside and when they were through they would put it back and even rebuild the stonewalls.

"Obviously that never happened," I said.

Bob nodded his head. "As a kid I loved passing this place. The green and yellow grasses crisscrossed by stonewalls made the fields look as if nature had covered them with a quilt."

I felt sad for the land, but especially for the house. Sitting in the middle of this scarred and ugly mess, it looked as deserted as an orphan.

Safe in the northwest corner, and not far from the house, was a little graveyard—the only evidence that life had mattered on this farm. We slowly walked over and by the time we'd reached its moss covered stonewalls, I felt as though I'd fallen in step with a procession of mourners. But, when I entered, instead of fresh earth the ground was a tangle of bittersweet and briars. There were fifteen or more headstones, eroded and encrusted with lichen; some were slate, some marble—worn and blurred by the passage of time. I squatted down and rubbed away the lichen on the face of a few: Joshua, Anna, Calab, Sarah. A baby, a husband, a wife. Deaths that ranged from 1725 to 1891. I looked up at the house. These were the people who had lived and died under its shelter.

I'd been too depressed by the land to pay much attention to the house, but now for the first time I gave it a good look. The asbestos shingles, windows with one-over-one sheets of glass, and a cinderblock chimney poking out of the roof indicated the 20th century. Except there was something about it that was different.

"It's the second floor gable-end overhang," Bob said.

"That's it," I replied. "That's 18th century construction. What are we standing here for?"

When we got closer, I noticed more details inconsistent with the 20th century. The foundation was granite instead of concrete, and the window frames protruded about two inches away from the walls just as they did in the 1700s. My heart raced. But when I looked through a window, all I could see were plywood floors, sheetrock walls and cardboard ceilings— material that matched the period of the asbestos shingles. Still, it was possible that this was a veneer—a 20th century attempt to modernize. If so, what was behind it? This could be a very old house, and considering the inferior site it was on, a house that might be slated for demolition. We looked at each other and nodded. Why bother the owner when we probably could find a way in now.

The front door was nailed shut and the windows sealed, but the skeleton key that Bob carried—for just this purpose— easily opened the back door. Without hesitation we walked into the kitchen. A damp, moldy smell filled our nostrils, and the only inhabitant was a scurrying mouse. I swept my eyes up the walls, across the ceiling and down to the floor looking for an exposed beam, a raised panel door, a fireplace, wide floor boards—anything that could give a hint of age—but like the room I'd seen through the window, every surface was covered in modern material.

But not the next room. Jumping and squealing as if I'd just won the lottery, I yelled at Bob to come see. A summer beam spanned the center of the ceiling, girts surrounded the top of the walls, and each corner had a post—exactly the kind of construction found in an early room. We were on to something special.

The door that led from this room to the next hadn't been used in so long that its seams were painted shut. Using a jackknife, Bob cut through the paint, and after a bit of fussing it came loose. I jiggled the door and it opened into a tiny front hall that had apple crates stacked to the ceiling. We shoved them aside and discovered a closed string stairway with a triple run that looked just like the pictures of ones I'd seen in a book about early houses. Despite many coats of cracked and peeling paint, it was magnificent. Its balusters were turned like the legs on a Windsor chair, the wall below the steps had a raised panel, and the area below the panel was finished in hand planed boards.

Excited, we continued to explore—the first floor, the second, the attic and the cellar—and wherever we looked we'd find more of its earliest parts hiding behind flimsy partitions. It was like Christmas morning. The jewel was a board-and-batten door. Its original butterfly hinges and wooden latch bar were still attached. The door was two boards wide with shadow moldings carved into the surface of the boards—a type of decoration out of fashion by 1690.

Shadow molding - cross section detail

I had been told that this kind of door would originally have been part of a wall decorated in the same manner, and I dared to believe that wall might still be waiting to be found behind the plastered walls. Even though the house was only giving out its secrets in whispers, we had learned enough to know that parts of it at least, were very old.

I kept pinching myself. How could this be possible? Here, in the middle of this castrated land, we'd found an ancient house with a story to tell and with a past to coax back. I was itching to get a tool and bust through its disguise. It would be like breaking open a piñata. I could already imagine its parts spilling out and into our lives. Not only was the house a perfect size for our whole family, it had all the old parts we loved. "Except," I said to Bob, "it will never work. No matter what we do it will still be sitting on a site that's outlived its meaning."

"Simple," he said. "We'll move it to another part of the land."

I knew that moving a whole house from one place to another wasn't a new idea. I'd heard stories about oxen hauling houses on rollers, and once I was caught in a traffic jam behind a house being towed down a street. I'd parked my car and gotten out to watch. Men were tying back branches and cutting telephone and electric wires so the house could advance. I remember thinking how cocky the house must feel as it passed by others forever stuck where they were. I was sure this house would feel just as smug if it was moved away from this desolate spot. Moving it seemed like a perfect solution. I looked at Bob and nodded YES.

"Let's go right now and find the owner," I said.

*   *   *

Now that saving the house seemed possible, I found myself switching from never wanting to see this farm again to worrying that it could have been sold since we talked with the owner four hours ago. I was relieved to find him at home and more relieved when he told us that so far there hadn't been much interest.

"It's the land," he said. "It's not much good for farming. A developer did come around, but I haven't heard from him for a while."

We told him we'd been in the house and liked it, but not its location. "We've been tossing around the possibility of moving it," Bob said, "provided there's an area on the farm that hasn't been destroyed."

"Interesting idea," the owner said. "There is a large undisturbed section. Come on, I'll walk the boundaries with you."

As we walked through a wooded area, the owner explained why this half of the farm had survived the gravel operation.

"Partly because of the woods here," he said, "but also because there's an Indian burial ground next to that field up ahead. When the bulldozer driver started to dig out gravel, he came up with a bucket full of bones. It scared the hell out of him and he left in a hurry. By the time another driver was hired the state didn't need any more gravel."

"Thank God," I said.

*　　*　　*

This part of the land included frontage on the river, a forest, a brook and a field—a perfect spot to locate the house and our lives. I could already imagine our days and nights cloaked by its ancient structure, waking in the morning and laughing with Bob at the bickering of busy sparrows, getting out of bed, my bare feet touching the silky knots in the ancient floor boards, and looking at my vegetable garden through the bubbles and waves in the hand blown window glass. A dream I was shaken from when we finally dared to ask the price. "Fifty-eight thousand," the owner replied. Not much for a house, river frontage and seventy acres of land by today's standards, but in 1967, a lot of money, and definitely more than we could afford.

"I have an idea," Bob said, and he looked at the owner. "We might be able to swing this if we could find a person who wanted to buy the barns and the graveled out section. Is that possible?"

"As a matter of fact," the owner replied, "there was a farmer who was particularly interested in the barns, but he'd been turned down when he'd applied for a farm loan. I remember him saying that the land was fine for his five hundred head of forced fed cattle. Holsteins, he'd said, a breed of milk machines that needed to be outside only when the barns are being cleaned. When we get back to my house, I'll give you his name."

The farmer was definitely interested in the part we didn't want, and tried again for a loan. A week later he called to say the loan had been approved. We shook hands on the deal, signed a bill of sale, and assured the farmer we'd call a house mover.

*   *   *

People who move houses don't live around the corner or even in the next town. The nearest company we could find, Metropolitan Building Movers, was located in Hyde Park, outside of Boston.

"We're pretty busy," I was told by the company's owner, a man named Roland. "It might be a couple of months, but I'll be in your area day after tomorrow and if you want I'll come over to Westport and take a look at the house and where it's going."

When Roland arrived in a green Cadillac, I expected to see a suit-and-tie guy get out of the car. Instead he had on a black and red checked lumberman's jacket, overalls and boots and looked about forty, the same age as Bob. Before he said hello, he stooped down and with a French Canadian accent spoke to our two youngest. I couldn't hear his words, but when he stood up they were giggling. Smiling, he said, "Hi, I'm Roland." He shook my hand and I could feel the roughness of hard work. I liked him right away.

"Nice house," he said. "Looks in good shape. Shouldn't be a problem to move it."

He told us he didn't have time to go inside. He'd do that later. "Right now," he said, "I need you to show me where it's going." Then he explained that it takes time to map out the route, get a moving permit and arrange for the telephone and electric company to be on hand to lower wires.

"It's only going next door," Bob said, "across that piece of land," and he pointed to what used to be a field.

Roland nodded. "That looks easy enough."

We walked across an open expanse to the edge of the woods and then into a meadow flaunting the soft greens of spring. Halfway down the edge of the meadow was the spot we'd chosen to put the house. It was next to a brook, near the forest, but out in the open enough to have gardens and maybe some sheep.

"I can see why you want to move the house over here. It's a beautiful spot," Roland said, then looked at a mile meter attached to his belt and told us the distance for the move was way under a mile.

"Actually the distance isn't what matters," he said. "It's getting it ready to move that does. I'm guessing, from the size of the house, it'll take us a week. It's now April. I think we can start the second week in June. You'll need that time to get in a well and have the foundation hole dug. And that's all I want—just a hole." And then he reminded Bob to be sure and tell the excavator that when he dug the hole he should leave one end open and level with the ground so the house could be backed in.

I asked him why we couldn't build the foundation first. He explained that if there was a foundation he wouldn't be able to back the house in because the foundation walls would be in the way of the trailer wheels.

"When the house is in place," Roland said, "I'll build some cribbing under the carrying beams and remove the wheels." He assured us the house would be just fine sitting that way until the foundation was built. When the foundation was ready, he'd come back, remove the beams and set the house down on its permanent foundation. I couldn't visualize it yet, but I was sure by the time the move was finished I would.

Fortunately—at least I thought so then—1967 was before perk tests were required, which gave us the freedom to simply go ahead and position the house without worrying about the water table. The front would face south as it always had. The east end would have a view of the river. The west end would be next to an old stonewall and close to the brook, and off the end of the house—to shield us from the north—we planned to build an ell. We also had to consider a driveway, where to park, and the placement of future outbuildings. Bob needed a boat shop. I needed a building for storing my collection of old house parts (now in a rented barn), and we both needed a place for storing tools. We juggled around imaginary structures until we were sure that the house and future buildings would work together as a family. Satisfied, we hammered stakes in the ground to outline the exact position of the house and the ell so a contractor would know where to excavate. While he was there, we'd also have him put in the parking area and our half mile driveway.

"It's got to wind through the woods and go over the brook with a wooden bridge," Bob said.

I loved that idea, especially the bridge and hearing the patter of wooden boards when I crossed in my car.

* * *

We hadn't told many friends about the house or that we

were planning to move it. We saw it as a great adventure but we doubted others would. We didn't need to hear, "My God, what a lot of work," or "You guys must be crazy." We already knew that. Still, word got out and friends drifted in. But instead of skeptics we had offers of help—from ripping off the asbestos shingles or photographing the whole process of moving and restoring, to taking care of the children whenever we needed them out of the way—and I had a feeling that that would be often. There was a huge amount of work to be done before we could even think about moving in.

* * *

There were still seven weeks before the house movers would appear, enough time for me to learn more about the house before it was moved. The previous owner knew nothing. He didn't even realize that the house was very old. Old to him was something that was falling apart. I did learn, at the local historical society, that John Goddard, the famous furniture maker, was born in the house in 1723. The only other reference to the house I could find was a will dated 1721, the year the owner had bequeathed it to his son. I felt sure its architectural details would tell us the rest, and I was anxious to start ripping off the 20th century veneer.

In the meantime I was having the usual mother pangs. The thought of picking up and moving a two story house with its chimney gave me the shivers. That had to be one heavy load. I kept thinking the more sheetrock, fake paneling, and bricks from the sealed up fireplaces that we got out of the house, the less it would weigh.

We removed its 20th century appendages very slowly, savoring each discovery—especially the Indian arrowhead I found buried in a crack, and a mark on the wall where another stairway had been. But Bob's discovery was the best. When he yelled to me to come see, I knew it would be special by the tone of his voice. I knew he'd been removing the bricks sealing up a fireplace but when I saw him I had to smile. Covered in soot, he looked like a charred piece of wood. When I looked through the opening he'd made and saw a series of fireplaces, I was flabbergasted. Three fireplaces— one inside the other. The last one was the first and earliest and was huge. It was like an inventory of change all the way back to the first page, but without any explanation.

Needless to say, by the time the movers appeared, we had more questions about the history of the house than answers.

*　　*　　*

House movers come with jacks, trucks, a front loader and a tractor, wood for cribbing, steel beams, wheels the size of a barn door, a crew of six, their own unique knowledge, and a guarantee that when the house is moved, it won't collapse. "It doesn't matter, brick, wood or stone," they advertise, "and if it's too big for the highway we'll cut it in half." Fortunately ours was only 30x40 feet, so that part wouldn't be necessary. Anyway our trip was across an open space and less than a mile.

When Roland arrived, he was all business. He parked his equipment, put his crew to work unloading his gear, and told us he was going to examine the house.

"If there are any weak areas, we'll have to fix them before it can be moved," he said.

He started in the cellar, and like a doctor he checked the underpinnings, then went from room to room checking every timber. Everything was okay until he got to the attic and discovered some joists had slipped out of their pockets.

"She's spread a bit over the years same as my grandmother," he said, and told us that to be on the safe side he was going to insert steel rods through her plate at four different places to make sure her front and back walls stayed together. He explained that each rod would have a turnbuckle that he would turn to tighten up the house.

"Don't want her collapsing on her first voyage," he said.

It sounded as though he was planning a hip operation. I didn't want to hear anymore. I put my hands over my ears and left, trusting that whatever he did would keep her safe.

While Roland and two other guys worked in the attic, the rest of the crew removed the earth from around the foundation. Two days later, when Roland announced, "That'll do," there was a 10x10 deep trench surrounding the house like a moat. Then he ordered his crew into the cellar to remove the foundation from under the chimney. This, Roland explained, had to be done so the part of the chimney from the first floor up could move with the house. Like miners, the men tunneled through the chimney's foundation, and as they dug out the rubble, they placed horizontal steel beams just below the hearth level. The beams, they said, would keep the upper part of the chimney from falling into the cellar. I was hurting for the house, but if it was going to have a new life obviously this was the only way.

*　*　*

Roland declared that now that the rods in the attic were in place he wanted to see our new foundation. As we walked over to the new site, he kept poking the ground with a shovel to see how firm it was.

"It's been a wet spring," he said. "There's nothing worse then getting a house stuck in the mud, but this seems okay." I couldn't resist asking him what he'd do if it was too wet.

"Bring in gravel," he said.

"Coals back to Newcastle," I muttered, and described to Roland what had happened to the land.

When we got to the site, Bob explained how we planned to build the foundation. We had decided it would cost too much to have all of it built in stone so we opted for a cinderblock base up to a foot below ground level. This way we would have enough space to finish the top with stone. We definitely didn't want to see cinderblock above ground where stones had always been.

"Good idea," Roland said and promised to save all the stones he could from the present foundation and bring them over in his truck. He told us the excavator had done a good job, but the area where the house would be backed into the hole would need a little more smoothing. "I'll send a guy over to fix that later today," he said.

*   *   *

After we returned to the house, Roland started the crew removing six-foot wide sections of the stone foundation. Each section was then  supported with cribbing—a stack of 6x6 timbers, crisscrossed on top of each other. When eight sections of the stone foundation had been replaced by eight stacks of cribbing, the rest of the foundation walls were knocked out. Balanced on stacks of cribbing, the house looked as if the slightest touch could push it over. I was relieved when Roland announced they were ready to start lifting. I wanted to get this over with.

The next day when I saw screw jacks next to the cribbing, I knew Roland was ready. As the crew slowly began to nudge it upwards—a little bit here, a little bit there—Roland circled the house checking for stress and talking to it like a trainer coaxing an elephant to stand. After the house had been raised eight inches, there was a gap between the top of the cribbing and the bottom of the sill, and I realized in horror that now the only supports for the house were the jacks. But not for long. The crew quickly filled the gaps with more cribbing timbers. This was a jacking process that would continue throughout the lifting.

I couldn't tell at what point Roland decided it was time for the hydraulic jacks, but they suddenly appeared to take over where the first jacks had left off. Once the hydraulic jacks were in place, the crew attached a hose to each one and then attached all the hoses to a master control panel as if the house was about to have an electrocardiogram.

When Roland flicked the switch on the control panel, rather than the house rising a little here and a little there as before, the whole house rose like an elevator and kept going up until he signaled enough and waved in a truck loaded with I-beams. Somehow, between a hoist and six men, they managed to get the carrying beams under the first floor of the house. After the beams were secured, four sets of huge wheels were rolled under the house and bolted to the beams. Like an illusion, the parts they'd attached to the underside of the house turned into a trailer—a trailer that eighty-three tons of house would ride on.

"We'll move it tomorrow," Roland announced, and then told me to be sure and put a full glass of water inside the door.

"If any spills before we reach the new foundation," he said, "you'll know we haven't done our job well." I didn't know if he was teasing, but I put the glass of water there anyway.

*   *   *

Dew was still on the ground when we arrived the next morning, but without any children. Worried they might get hurt, we had left them behind with a baby sitter. Roland and his crew were already there, and it wasn't long before we attracted a crowd of camera-carrying people. Friends we had called, our new neighbors and various others who had heard that a house was on the move—a cheering section of fifteen or so people. Even the man we'd bought the property from showed up. He came with his wife and they both kept staring at the house not knowing what to make of it—but neither did I. With the wheels underneath it, it was high off the ground and looked as if it was floating on the early morning mist.

Some thoughtful person was passing around coffee and donuts, but I was too nervous to think about putting anything in my stomach. Bob gave me a hug and told me everything would be fine. "Roland knows what he's doing," he said. "Stop worrying."

But that was impossible. If nobody else was going to worry then I certainly had to. I couldn't take my eyes off Roland as he performed a final check—the air pressure of the tires, the bolts that held the trailer to the house, and then the bar for attaching the trailer to the tractor. When he was finished, he signaled to the tractor driver to back up to the house. Then the tractor and the house were hitched together.

It isn't every day that a house takes a walk. I was torn between fear and pride, like watching a child about to take its first step, and I jumped when Roland spun his fist, pierced the air with a thrust, and shouted, "Roll it." The tractor's engine revved and as the house slowly moved forward—ever so gently being nudged from its roots—my throat caught and I had to turn my back for a moment.

The sound of clicking cameras filled the air, but after forty feet the forward motion came to a halt and there was sudden quiet. The house had arrived at a place where the ground dropped away—a hill a sledder might like, but not an old house. I looked at the house and then at the hill. I couldn't imagine how it could get to the bottom without landing in a nosedive. House anxiety gripped my stomach. Bob anxiously puffed on his pipe while Roland lit a cigarette with a "no problem" look on his face. He must know how to handle this, I thought, after all it was his business, but I couldn't help thinking this definitely had the makings of a suicide leap.

I watched as Roland took some measurements, checked the hitch, then signaled to his crew. They grabbed some jacks, pumped up the front end of the house, and now the house looked like a cannon about to be fired. Roland, seeing my face turn ashen, came over to explain that in order to get the house down the hill it had to be kept level or it would collapse in on itself. I understood, but still didn't like any part of it. I held my breath when they jumped in the truck and started the engine. The house crept forward—inch by inch. Then every few feet they'd stop again to level it—a nerve wracking process that continued all the way down the hill.

Finally, at the bottom, when the house looked normal again—at least as normal as an old house can look perched on a trailer—I did the only thing left to do—I shrieked. Roland had kept his promise. I looked at the glass sitting in the doorway. Not a drop of water had spilled.

*   *   *

It was mid-afternoon. Nobody had eaten, but nobody cared. The crew, our friends, Bob and I were just happy knowing that flat ground was ahead and our destination in sight. Freed of tension and feeling a bit goofy, we celebrated by dancing along beside the house waving our jackets like flags and making up songs about an old house on an afternoon outing, happily chaperoning it across the land to reach its new life. Even Roland joined in, his crew stupefied by his actions but unable to stop a rhythmical clapping. By sundown our house had been settled in its new location and looked idyllic—under the trees and next to the brook. No doubt, after we said good night, the deer, fox and raccoons wandered out to meet the new creature that had entered their woods.

Fitting In

Dawn, trickling through the hatch, woke me. I sprang to an upright position, rubbed my eyes and looked around. Yes, this was our boat. Yes, this was our stateroom, and yes, Bob was asleep beside me. Okay, I'd only been dreaming. We had not moved seven buildings to our site yesterday, only one. But the dream had seemed so real that for a moment I'd thought about waking Bob. I lay down, rolled over and smiled. Of course we'd only moved one. One extraordinary house, its architecture more baffling than any dream I could ever have. I lay there and for the umpteenth time tried to interpret what I'd discovered as an archeologist tries to interpret remains.

At this point the only two things I was sure of were that the house was on the site by 1721, and that it was a two story center chimney Georgian that began as a two story 'half house'—a sliced down the middle Georgian—before the other side had been added.

I knew this because of the double posts near the middle of the house. Joining the posts of one building to the posts of another was a common 18th century method for attaching an addition. And by the locations of these double posts, I could even tell which side had been built first. All very obvious. After all I

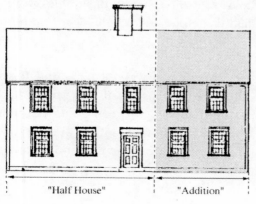

"Half House"   "Addition"

was the old house expert, at least that's what I'd thought until the house beckoned me into the attic.

The board wall, that had been the sheathing for the outside end wall before the second section had been added, was still in place. I was delighted. The wall even lined up with the double posts, confirming my theory that the house indeed had started out as a 'half house'. Curious or maybe just to say "hello" to the faithful old boards, I waved my flashlight across the side of the wall that faced the inside of the original house. Then I looked on the reverse side of the wall, and when I noticed the imprint of two angled lines on the boards I knew, like a bloodhound, that I had just picked up an important scent. Using the beam of my flashlight as a pointer, I followed the path of the imprint up the board wall and was stunned when I realized that I was looking at an imprint of a roof line that had belonged to a one story house. Had the one story house been the first house on the site or was it simply the first addition to the two story half house? Then again this one story thing could have had a second story added before the other half of the house had been built. But if that was true it would mean that what I thought was the first side was really the second.

I rolled over in my bed and kept on thinking.

For sure, both sides of the boards couldn't be exterior walls at the same time. In order to know which side was which, I had looked for nail holes where clapboards or shingles would have been. But that hadn't helped—nail holes were on both sides.

I rolled over again.

I remembered that when I had walked back and forth searching for more clues on either side of the wall, I had suddenly realized that the doorway I'd been going through wasn't a doorway at all. It had been a window. A piece of the window frame was still attached to the opening and its other pieces were now framing the trap door at the top of the ladder that led to the roof.

My head pounded.

That had been confusing enough, but it had gotten worse when I'd noticed that the rafters for the side that I thought had been the first half of the house each had pieces of wood, eighteen inches long, scarfed into their peak ends to make them longer. Had this been a smaller roof? Had these rafters come from another roof? Or had the carpenter simply fixed a measurement goof?

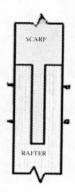

I curled into a fetal position and remembered how, just when I thought I'd reached a dead end, I'd discovered that one edge of the collars (beams that serve as braces to keep the roof from sagging) had notches every eight inches, presumably to hold the sticks that thatching is tied to. That meant that these collars had once been 17th century rafters, predating everything else except for the shadow molded door that was now in the opening where the window had been.

The door was the same door that I'd found earlier, except since then I'd discovered matching boards with the identical shadow molding. So now it seemed that if I bundled the door with the boards and the collars—that had once been rafters—I would have a 17th century house with no place to put it. Unless—yes, it was possible—these were the parts from the one story house that wasn't there anymore.

I pulled the pillow over my head.

Would I ever figure this out? I lay there for a moment longer. Maybe tomorrow or the day after. If there was anything more to learn, I'd never learn it by lying in bed. In the meantime the house's story was safely stored in its attic.

I kicked off the covers. This was the day after the day of moving our house, and the day to get started turning it into our home.

I dressed our two youngest and hurried them across the deck to the galley. My five oldest children had gone to England to be with their father. I missed them terribly, but on the other hand having fewer children around meant more time to work on the house. It was a calm morning, the boat was still, and for the moment I didn't have to worry about our two and four-year-old falling overboard. What a joy it will be, I thought, when I can open a door and let them run free, but I knew it would be more than a year before we could move in. The house needed a major overhaul inside and out.

We gathered up toys and children, lunches to travel, lists, rulers, pencils, and jumped in our truck—the start of a thirty minute daily commute from Warren to Westport.

*   *   *

Our house was just as we'd left it but with a look of expectancy as if saying, "Now what?"—and the reality of the amount of work ahead suddenly sank in. As I toured the house, up and down, inside and out, the "r" words roared through my head—repair, restore, reclaim—and I could see that rulers, paper and pencils would be of little use except to figure how many shingles were needed. There was a foundation to finish, structural repairs to make, window sash to replace, a chimney top to rebuild, asbestos siding to remove, roof and walls to shingle, and trim to paint.

The inside was still a mess. We'd pulled the acoustical tiles and veneers off the ceilings and walls, but the plaster underneath was cracked and full of nail holes. Five fireplaces needed re-pointing. Sheets of plywood covering the floor boards had to be pulled up. There was wallpaper and peeling paint to strip off, woodwork to patch, plumbing, heating, and electricity to install. Repairs and installations that would take care of its aches and pains and our practical needs, but not its soul.

I felt as if we'd adopted a foster child, a hand-me-down from the day its first piece had been cut out of the forest. Since then it had been through many changes with a past that was lying around everywhere, as if a suitcase of clothes had been dumped on the floor. But not its future—that was in our hands—and as surrogate parents we had a lot to think about. I grabbed an apple crate, upended it, and sat down.

Would the house mind if we took out a partition, put in a sliding glass door, shelves for the tons of books we owned, a second stairway? Which room could be used as a kitchen, a bathroom, a living room, a dining room, a library, a master bedroom, children's rooms? What kind of heat could we use, and what about closets? There weren't any.

Turning it into a museum was out of the question. We wanted to live in the house, not tiptoe around a stage setting. I loved the idea of plumbing, heating and electricity. I certainly wasn't about to give up a tub of hot water, my refrigerator for an ice chest, a gas stove for an open fire, or a radiator to dry my mittens on, and I definitely wanted a freezer for all the vegetables I would be growing—canning wasn't for me. Anyway the house had already proved it had an amazing ability to adapt to all the centuries. After all, it wouldn't still be here if it hadn't. I grinned. I loved this house.

"What are you smiling at?" Bob asked when he came into the room.

"The house and I've been bonding," I replied, then laughed and stood up. "I was feeling happy for our house. It could have been gutted or torn down, instead it's still here and ready for us to give it a future."

We walked through the rooms, trying out their moods, trying to get a sense of them, and it wasn't long before we knew which room would be best to use for what. The first floor had six rooms, two large ones in the front and four across the back. The two rooms in the front would stay as they were—one a dining room and the other a living room. Of the four rooms across the back, one was a perfect size for a bathroom. Another was large enough for a library with a second stairway in its corner. But each of the other two rooms was too small for a kitchen unless we removed a partition. Structurally, it wouldn't harm the house, historically it wasn't significant, but spiritually it did mean taking away a part of its past. We decided that would be okay as long as we documented what we had done in the journal we were keeping about the house.

We were both enchanted with the idea of replacing a window in the kitchen with a sliding glass door—two pieces of clear glass that would let us step into the outside and the outside step inside to us. I wasn't worried about how it would look. Its clean functional lines were as true as the frame of the house. As for the 'old house purists'—I'd simply tell them this was our own piece of history, our footprint, for somebody in the future to wonder about.

The upstairs was perfectly arranged for five bedrooms and even a bathroom. When all the kids were home, there'd be some doubling, but not jammed like living on a boat. And closets? They'd just have to wait until we figured out how to squeeze them in somewhere, somehow.

While we were walking through the house, the children had discovered that the rooms circled the chimney. Screaming with delight they ran through the rooms, around and around the chimney, dissolving in a fit of giggling when they bumped into each other. But the chimney, other than entertainment for kids, had a real purpose. It was the central heating system. Back in the days when fireplaces were used continuously, the heat would be absorbed by all the bricks in the chimney turning the entire stack into a radiator—a good reason why many old houses were built with the chimney in the center. Even with the small fire we'd made to heat up some water, the bricks were warm to the touch. Who decided our forefathers were cold? This was the best heating system going—if one was willing to cut, split and dry the wood to keep a fire continually burning. Not us. Other than an evening fire to take off the chill, Bob and I had other things to do. We wanted a furnace.

We liked hot air heat. It warmed the house up fast, but as Bob pointed out, it would be impossible to run duct work through the thin walls of an 18th century house. The alternative was hot water heat that circulates through small pipes to either old fashioned radiators or new finagled baseboards. But we agreed that covering the house's wooden baseboards with metal heating units would destroy a harmony. The baseboards, posts and girts, when painted the same color, outline a wall as a frame outlines a portrait. "It'll have to be stand-alone radiators," Bob said, and reminded me that they were great for warming one's butt. By the time we'd walked through each room, discussed its personalities and needs, and returned to the first floor, we knew how to fit in. It was time to get to work.

But the house was still sitting the way Roland had left it and nothing could be done on the inside or the outside until we built the foundation. The next day instead of pencils and paper we brought a truckload of cinderblocks, bags of mortar, buckets, hammers and chisels. While I mixed the mortar, Bob worked on the foundation. We planned to build the cinderblock walls five feet tall, followed by twelve inches of stone of which eight would show above ground. Laying the cinderblock went fairly fast but not the stonework. Roland had delivered the original stones from the foundation as promised, even the door stones, but digging through the pile to find the right stones, then splitting and fitting them together was a long tedious job. What was particularly time consuming was laying the last row of stones. They had to be absolutely even so the house would sit level when lowered.

Three weeks later we were ready to call Roland. He was delighted, as he was in the process of moving three other houses and needed his beams that were still under our house. He arrived the next day, jacked the house up, removed the cribbing, pulled out the beams, and lowered it down. Snug on its new foundation, our house was ready to grow its roots.

After Roland left we walked out to the field to look back at the house. It looked perfect, as if it had always been there.

"A little lonely though," Bob said, and he turned me sideways.

"Look over there."

I looked. All I could see was a field.

"It's field now but remember the plans we had for a storage shed?"

I nodded, and he pointed to the spot we had chosen.

"Before Roland left he told me about a shed in Marshfield, Massachusetts, that's going to be demolished."

As I remembered my dream about seven buildings, I felt a prickly feeling run up my spine. All I could say was, "So soon?"

"I know," Bob said, "but it's not just any old shed. It's one of a kind." And he explained that the shed had belonged to a shipbuilder and was the only remaining building on the site of his pre-Revolutionary shipyard. Then he grinned, pulled out his tobacco pouch, filled his pipe, struck a wooden match and drew in.

"There's no harm in looking," he said. "If we like it we can always move it here on our trailer."

And I thought *I* had the old house disease!

The next day we drove to Marshfield, and the instant I saw the shed I fell in love. There was no question that it had to be saved. It was one story tall with a steep roof pitch, two little windows, four posts shaped like a gunstock, wide vertical oak sheathing, plus six sets of hewn rafters, and a huge gable-end door. Its history was special, its proportions beautiful, and its construction straightforward, as if it was saying, "I am what I am." A perfect companion for our house. The only problem—the land developer wanted it out of there immediately. It was 12x14 feet, and much too big for our trailer.

"Easy to dismantle," Bob said. "We'll bring it home piece by piece."

It took three days. Not because it was difficult, it wasn't, but because we had our two and four-year-old in tow, and an hour and a half road trip up and back. We'd pack a lunch, get to the site around ten, work a few hours, keep the children entertained removing their own patch of shingles, have a picnic lunch, work some more while the children were napping, then load the truck with the parts we'd removed, head to Westport, unload, go back to our boat, get everybody fed, the kids washed and into bed. The shed had a better life than we did.

Three weeks later the shed had claimed its spot in the field. Re-erected, shingled and the trim painted, it was perfect—fitting in exactly as planned. It was close enough to the house to be its offspring, but far enough away to remain its own person. The only thing left to do was to hang its gable-end door. I could see by a mark that the door originally had been hung with strap hinges. That was not unusual, but the fact that the hinges had been five feet long was—and finding a pair of five foot strap hinges would be next to impossible unless we had them made.

"I have one," I told Bob. "I found it in a cellar years ago, but I never found its mate."

"Believe it or not, I think I have the other," he said. And when we laid them together we had a matching pair.

Coincidence? Who knows, but attaching them to the door was like passing rings and getting married all over again. In fact it was better.

*   *   *

It was late July and I was keeping my fingers crossed in hopes that no more buildings would arrive before we had a chance to start on the house. But I knew my dream was still hanging around when Bob announced there was water in the cellar. I suppose it was better to find out now rather than later that the house was sitting on a floodplain, that the cellar would be of little use except for wading. That meant we'd definitely need an ell sooner than planned. The ell would have to hold our furnace and all the other things one normally delegates to a cellar. Bob already owned a building in Westport that he no longer used. Originally the building had been a little two room house which he'd converted to use as his workshop and office. We hadn't thought about using it as our ell, but now it seemed like the perfect solution. It was about one hundred and fifty years old, one story tall. One half would be the furnace room and the other a bedroom.

We called Roland and fortunately caught him between jobs. "It'll be a snap to move," he said when he came to look. He told us that as soon as he got a permit to move it the eight miles from Westport Point to Drift Road he'd be back. This time he told us we could build the foundation walls first. The building was small enough to straddle with his wheels.

Three weeks later the building was sitting on its new foundation. I'd like to say it was perfect but it wasn't—it was two feet too short—a blooper that we couldn't blame on a tape measure. So what. Adding two extra feet to the ell meant more space on the inside.

I had to admit that moving three buildings in eight weeks was record breaking. A friend asked if we were running a shelter for homeless houses and another friend suggested we think about planned parenthood. I chuckled and agreed we were producing buildings faster then a housing development. On the other hand, if my dream of seven buildings was some kind of prophecy, the next arrival was inevitable.

* * *

By late August we finally had time to work on the house. We set up staging and started to rip off the asbestos shingles.

They were a bitch to get off. Nailed on top of wooden ones, they refused to loosen; they'd snap, slide down my bar, de-flesh my knuckles, and then fall to the ground in a million pieces. Not a fun beginning, but it improved when we started ripping off the wooden ones and Bob found a shingle with "W.S.B. Reshingled. 1882," penciled on the back. When Bob showed me the shingle, I felt an instant connection. W.S.B, whoever he was, had been taking care of the house, the same as we were, but almost one hundred years ago.

Then, when all the shingles were heaped on the ground like a pile of cast-off clothing, a forgotten time appeared. The sheathing under the shingles was patched like somebody's old underwear. There was a patch where a door had been, a patch where a window had been, and a patch where once there had been an addition. Pit saw marks, band saw marks, and circular saw marks on the sheathing gave more clues as to when some of the changes had happened. We might never have the answers as to why or who made these changes, but what we did have was the creaking sound of the house breathing when we walked across the floor, the hand split lath that caused the plaster to ripple with shadows, pottery shards that lurked in the cracks, corncobs in the walls, and the mysteries in the attic—the life of the house that would have been lost if it had been dismantled instead of moved.

*　*　*

By the way my dream was unfolding I wasn't surprised when an 18th century slaughter shack from Cranston, Rhode Island, that I was hired to dismantle ended up in my own backyard. The Newport Restoration Foundation had wanted to use the building as part of a permanent exhibit of a 1750s working-farm "the way it was" sort of thing. But not long after I delivered the building and got paid for my work, the Foundation canceled their plans and offered to sell me the building for a dollar—"To make it legal," the director had said. An irresistible offer, and building number four arrived.

Somehow, despite adopting buildings, we had managed to keep working on the house. By the end of October we had rebuilt the chimney top, shingled the roof and walls, and even painted the trim. The only thing left to do before we could declare the outside finished was to replace the 20th century double-hung, single-pane window sash with 18th century double-hung

I planned to use sash from my collection of old house parts, but before the sash could be installed they needed to be stripped of their paint, soaked in linseed oil, then each pane reset and glazed—seven hundred and seventy-four panes of glass—a huge job that I was saving for winter. However, now that the house looked almost perfect I couldn't resist getting at least enough sash ready for the front of the house.

After the sash was in place, I stood back to take a look. Dressed in all its proper clothes the house smiled back and if my arms had been long enough I would have given it a hug. The rebuilt chimney, now the proper size to handle the business of smoke, no longer looked like a thimble on top of the roof. The new shingles flowed across the wall as if they were dancing to a delicate rhythm. Shadows cast by the window frames made them seem to float. The many-paned sash sparkled in the sunlight instead of having black eyes. And because the inside frame—the posts, girts and rafters— were now outlined by the outside corner, fascia, and rack boards, the invisible had become visible. But it wasn't only light, shadows and patterns that looked spectacular—the windows, doors, and chimney top, and even each pane of glass were in perfect proportion with the overall proportions of the house. The house looked radiant.

I had never thought about what makes an old house glow

until Bob said, "It was designed and built by instinct, not by architects."

That was it. The shape, the size, the individual details had been created by gut feeling. Something the old time builders knew how to do which today is forgotten.

* * *

Now that four buildings were happily putting down roots, Bob was anxious to get back to his boat shop and I was itching to start on the inside of the house. Over the years I'd learned how to take apart, repair, and put houses back together, and now at age thirty-eight I had a decent pair of carpenter's hands. Except I made sure Bob understood that this carpenter never touched plumbing, heating or electricity—that would have to be his baby. Anyway at this point I didn't need electricity, just good old fashioned tools. I hated power tools, I hated the noise, but most of all they scared me to death.

Some of the work was monotonous—stripping paint, patching plaster, installing insulation, pulling up plywood. Some was utterly satisfying—replacing a missing part in an old piece of wood with a dutchman, fitting in a stairway, replacing a missing chimney breast and a corner cupboard with ones I'd saved from another house, scribing and fitting to a wall the remnants of the shadow molded boards so they wouldn't be forgotten, building a hutch in the kitchen to hold our dishes, saving the sagging ceiling by screwing the plaster and lath back to the joists.

And as I worked on the house, its past kept appearing, like aunts and uncles and distant relatives arriving unexpectedly for Thanksgiving. The missing panel above the huge fireplace was in the attic recycled as a floor board. The original first floor doors were hiding under the eaves. The cupboard doors from a chimney breast were stuffed behind a wall, and an entire room of feather boards was hiding under plaster in the room we had planed to use as a bathroom.

Too special for such a use, it became an office or rather that's what we decided to call it.

*　*　*

Two years had gone by since the first building arrived. Moving, dismantling and putting back together three more—the shed, the ell, an outbuilding—while trying to earn a living in between—meant that the house was far from finished. But we sold our boat and moved in anyway, even though Bob would no longer have a boat shop. He'd been using a building on the wharf where our boat had been tied, but without a boat the building was no longer available—an excellent excuse for acquiring another building.

And when someone called and told us about a house on Russell's Mill Road in Dartmouth, Massachusetts, that was in the way of a bulldozer naturally we had to look. It was a 1790s one story house, and a perfect size for a boat shop. Not only did its construction meet the needs for a shop, it had a lot of excellent interior woodwork. The demand for house parts had increased tenfold and as fast as we could take out its interior, the parts were sold. Building number five was actually paying us to give it a home. Not only did bills get paid, we had enough leftover to buy our house a necklace in the shape of a stonewall.

We still needed a barn. Not for cows or horses but for all my house parts stored elsewhere. I no longer questioned where to find one. They seemed to find us. And building number six arrived. A beautiful big barn from Gloucester, Rhode Island, with hewn timbers, three bays, and a loft above. After dismantling and putting it back up, we had plenty of room to store whole houses.

*　*　*

Two more years went by. Every once in a while I

remembered my dream and wondered what happened to number seven, but now that we had all the buildings we wanted I chased the thought away.

Then how, I've asked myself, did I end up with number seven? Maybe because, like a hitchhiker, the house was standing alone by the side of a road in East Providence, Rhode Island. The road was about to be widened, and the house would have been run over if I hadn't stopped to pick it up. But I suspect the real reason was that it was a perfect, small, one story, 17th century Rhode Island stone-ender that I didn't want anybody else to have. For reasons I don't yet understand—perhaps I lived in one in another life—a Rhode Island 17th century stone-ender has always been closest to my 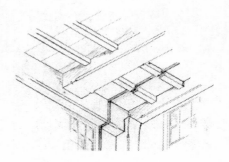 heart. Although the stone end on this house had been removed years ago, its frame was still perfect: the fat oak timbers were chamfered, the joists were planed smooth, and the huge summer beam running down the middle of the ceiling was so special that it was worth bumping one's head on.

Moving the house on wheels was out of the question. It would have to pass through four towns, requiring four different permits which could take weeks to acquire, and the road builders wanted it out of there yesterday. Sometimes it's useful being a woman. I smiled and asked for four days and they gave me a week.

My crew and I agreed that if we couldn't move it intact we should try to take it apart in sections—something we had never done. First we took out the pegs that held the rafters together at the peak of the roof. Then as a unit—rafters, roof boards and shingles—we lifted off each side of the roof with a crane and laid it flat on a trailer. The exterior walls, attached to studs, were removed next in the same way as the roof. When all the walls were stacked on the trailer, the only thing left standing was a big, beautiful, gorgeous frame, which we then disassembled. Five days later the frame, the walls, the roof, arrived in Westport intact, and a month later, when we put the house back up, all the pieces fit together perfectly.

The house sits in a quiet place of its own—across the brook, sheltered by a canopy of trees. It has no practical purpose. It's like a chapel in the woods, a place to go, a place to sit quietly, a place where the past is part of the present.

My dream was no longer a dream. It had become "Bakerville." Our house and its six siblings had wrapped their arms around us. As adoptive parents we had been good to all of them, and there was no question that they had taught me more than I had taught them.

Upheaval

While Bakerville had been growing, so had the public's interest in preservation. By the early 70s it seemed everybody wanted to own, restore or move an old house. I had no idea what had sparked the interest until I learned that a few years earlier the National Trust for Historic Preservation had joined with the federal government to establish a Preservation Act. The Act consisted of a National Registry, a sort of Who's Who for historically important structures; the appointment of historical commissions to perform historic surveys and oversee restoration work; a set of guidelines for restoration do's and don'ts; and a promise of grant money and tax credits to accelerate interest. I was delighted. At last our government realized that urban renewal, shopping malls, freeways, and housing developments were eating up our old houses.

And the timing was perfect. The nation was ready for something new to think about. The hippie movement had faded. Smoking, abortion, and gun control were still not an issue and the bicentennial was creeping up with little to show about our built environment. Whatever the reason, the word 'preservation' was on everybody's lips—first as a mumble, then a chant and before long a full call to action, as if a cultural revolution had changed the way everybody thought about our architectural heritage.

I, too, was swept into the frenzy. People needed an architectural historian, a contractor, antique building material, or advice. At first I thought fantastic, no more demoed or sacked houses, until I realized that the National Trust—with all its rules, regulations, and promises—had forgotten to mention that an old house needs love, understanding, and patience: the knots in the floor boards stick up like knuckles;

favorite pieces of furniture won't fit up the stairway; a box spring won't go up either. Instead of coils embedded in cozy, soft fibers, the box spring has to be a 4x8 sheet of plywood cut in half to get up the stairway. Low doorways threaten foreheads, and if the guests don't hit their heads they'll probably get their clothes caught on wrought-iron door latches. Tables need wedges to keep them level, and if the kids play marbles you'll soon hear them screaming as the marbles roll into a mouse hole. The smell of old shoes can't be eradicated. Petrified dirt is wedged between the cracks. The only bathroom is under the stairs and you can't bend over. And don't expect to hang up your clothes—there aren't any closets.

Finding a huge dumpster parked in front of an old house wasn't unusual. If the dumpster was filled with stuff from the 40s—lace curtains, shag rugs, linoleum from the kitchen, and a collection of magazines from the attic—I was relieved. But when it was filled with bricks, beams, and old boards, I knew the owners had lost their patience and hired an architect to redesign history. Architects hadn't been taught about the old way of seeing—rooms were enlarged for entertainment centers, doorways expanded to accommodate six-foot-eight people, stairways widened to accommodate kingsize mattresses, fireplaces replaced by bathrooms and closets, and floors machine sanded, turning generations of footsteps into sawdust.

Contractors hired to do the work didn't understand that an old house had a voice. Roofs were replaced when contractors discovered rafters were spaced four feet on center—even though after two hundred and fifty years the roof wasn't sagging. Exterior walls were given a layer of plywood to keep the house from swaying—even though swaying was how an old house outwitted a hurricane. Clapboards were replaced by vinyl siding even though vinyl siding kept the house from breathing. Doors were given a third hinge to keep them from warping—even though the doors were straight as a pin and a third hinge had never been needed. Beams were drilled with holes for plumbing and heating pipes—even though they were the bones the house relied on. Some contractors even convinced owners to tear the house down and build a reproduction. Others covered their inexperience by charging double the usual amount—and owners who loved their house decided they no longer could afford it.

The National Trust's rules were just as upsetting. I couldn't understand why they were saying a house should be restored to its original period. This meant destroying its life's story. I couldn't understand why they thought that the only thing important was the shape, the date and if somebody famous had owned the house—which would eliminate 90% of houses needing understanding. I couldn't understand why they said a repair must match the original feature in design texture and visual qualities. This meant that if a section of a beam had to be replaced, it would have to be hand hewn and stained brown. For me nothing is more beautiful than an honest repair. I learned that when Bob repaired the rotted end of an exposed timber at Bakerville. Using modern tools and matching wood, he joined the new to the old. There were no adze marks and he didn't stain it dark brown to make it look like something it wasn't. Every time I looked at it, I was reminded that the 20th century has a story to tell also.

*   *   *

By the mid 70s the marketplace had expanded to meet the demands of preservation. There were books and magazines on everything one needed to know about do-it-yourself restoring. There were stores that supplied historic products: furniture and furnishings, lighting, hardware, plumbing fixtures, old fashioned paint colors, and all kinds of new glues to make the job easier. There were woodworking mills that advertised old type windows, doors, entries, mantles, and stairways. There were architects and contractors who added the words preservation/restoration to their business cards, and landscapers who added the words old fashioned gardens. There were real estate companies who doubled the price for structures more than one hundred years old and second-hand dealers who doubled their price for antique house parts. And for those who didn't want a genuine old house, there were post and beam reproductions. And if a person liked the idea of an old house, but didn't want to live in one, there were styrofoam beams, stained brown, that could be glued to the ceiling.

During this time rumors of grant money for restoring old houses had spread, but few people bothered to read the fine print. The money applied only to houses eligible for the National Registry—architecturally pure, or a George Washington type person had slept there. For houses that did pass the test, the owner soon found out that the promise of grant money depended on how much the local historical commission had in their kitty—which sometimes wasn't any. But even worse, if the money was available the owner had to put the work out to bid, and only the historical commission could choose the contractor even though they didn't know how to determine if a contractor understood old houses.

Not everybody wanted to be on the Registry, and most houses didn't qualify, but that didn't stop some people from becoming neurotic. I had one client who was so nervous about the National Trust's guidelines that she asked me if I thought it would be more in keeping with the period of her house if she and her husband switched to single beds.

As the momentum grew, old houses became a commodity, and for some, a tax shelter. In Newport, Rhode Island, a bunch of ancient and orphaned houses, sixty in all, were hastily acquired by a newly established restoration foundation. This could have benefited many old houses, but the project was at the whim of an heiress and a hired director, whose only degree was in European cathedrals. Houses were shuffled around, torn apart, pieces amputated and attached to others, until little was left of their original bodies. The houses were then painted red, green and yellow and given a plaque that said they were old. Newport had become a giant stage setting.

Then there were private individuals who wanted to dismantle and move an old house to their upscale neighborhood. One man combed the countryside and ended up with two. "Trophies of a successful hunt. I wanted to get them before anybody else did," he told me.

Then he admitted he didn't need two, but figured he'd use the parts from one to make the other one larger. He didn't care that both were rare 17th century Rhode Island stone-enders—one in Portsmouth and the other in Tiverton—that could have stayed where they were.

The state historical commissions were supposed to prevent these kinds of atrocity, but like the Asian flu, the Preservation Act had appeared so suddenly that there hadn't been time for the commission members to learn how to recognize what was old and what wasn't.

Consequently courses in regional architecture began to pop up everywhere. Some offered a degree after only six weeks of study—a degree that didn't include touching the parts of a house, recognizing changes and understanding a housewright by his joinery methods and scribe marks. Instead students learned how to recognize Colonial, Federal, Greek Revival, and Victorian structures by their façade, not by what was behind their walls.

A graduate who was appointed to the historical commission was told to survey a house in the path of a road. He looked at the outside, declared it Victorian and okayed the demolition. I looked inside and discovered it was 17th century.

Another house was declared a National Registry candidate—a rare example of a tiny stone house. If the commission member had been taught what to look for, he would have known that it was a pigsty.

Those of us who had learned by doing knew much more than could be taught in a classroom. However, since we had no degree to prove our knowledge, the historical commission was not allowed to seek our advice.

Some people didn't want advice. They had read the do-it-yourself books on how to make a house look authentic. This created a demand for antique building material. Midnight salvage from empty old houses became a new kind of vandalism. I arrived one morning at a house I was preparing to move and found that three mantles had been stolen. I was horrified and worried that the burglars would probably be back for the doors, the hardware, and the wide board flooring. I tacked up a sign.

> **POISON**
> **DANGER**
> **Premises**
> **treated with a**
> **HIGHLY TOXIC RODENTICIDE**

And nothing more went missing.

But I have to admit I did my own share of vandalizing. I called it liberating. My friends laughed at me, "Is there a difference?"

"Of course," I'd reply, and then explain by telling them about an empty house that was smack in the middle of farmland where a developer was planning to build a mall. The house, built in the early 1700s, was two stories with an end chimney and a beautiful exposed frame. I knew damn well it would be demolished. I went to the town hall and found out the developer's name—a big shot who worked out of New York City. I wrote him a letter to tell him that if he intended to get rid of the house, I would be interested in moving it off the site. I offered him two hundred dollars, assured him the dismantling would be at my own risk, and all the other kind of stuff lawyers tell one to put in writing. He didn't answer.

I tried calling.

I wrote again.

I raised my offer.

I called again.

He never responded.

Then one day yellow stakes appeared and I knew the bulldozers weren't far behind. The next weekend, with a bunch of friends and as many trucks, we dismantled the house, loaded the parts into the trucks and drove away. By Sunday night the only thing left in the yard was an old walnut tree.

Then, just to make sure my friends understood the difference between stealing and liberating, I told them about an abandoned house in the path of an Industrial Park. Its roof was caving in and the windows smashed. The insides had been stripped of all the woodwork except for a room of vertical wall boards. The boards were beautiful--eighteen inches wide, hand planed with a bevel on each edge that fitted into a beaded grove on the next board, and so on around the room as if the boards were holding hands.

There was no question that these boards needed to be rescued and soon—before the house fell down. I found out the name of the owner and called him. He was in one of those 'meetings' so I gave the secretary my name and told her about the house and my interest in buying the boards. She assured me she would tell him and he would get back to me. Either he stayed in the meeting for six months or the secretary forgot, because each time I called I was told he was in a meeting, but would get back to me.

I visited the boards every so often to tell them I was working on saving them, but one morning when I woke to a downpour, I said to myself, that's it, those boards have been out in the open long enough. I packed the children off to school, got into my truck, drove to the house, and backed up to the front door—liberating also meant getting in and out as fast as I could. However, I soon discovered why the boards had never been taken. A later ceiling had been installed below their tops and there was no way of freeing them without first removing the ceiling.

The ceiling was held up by faring strips—thin wooden strips that were nailed across the room for attaching lath and plaster. I suspected that if I loosened the strips the weight of the plaster would pull down the ceiling. Standing on the girts above the ceiling, I worked my way around the edges loosening the faring strips as I went. The ceiling started to sag, but it was taking too long, and I was getting nervous that I would be discovered. I sat down on the edge of a girt, raised my foot and slammed it down on the ceiling. It fell and broke into a million pieces. The noise was horrendous followed by clouds of plaster dust that rose out of the roof. To a neighbor it would look as if the house was on fire, and minutes later I heard a police siren. My first instinct was to take my tools and run. But no, the boards and I were in this together. I dropped my tools and walked out the door. Before the policeman had a chance to say anything I told him my name.

"It's not smoke," I said. "It's just plaster dust. Didn't mean to worry you."

I explained that I had just knocked down a ceiling so I could remove some boards. I told him they were beautiful old boards, and asked him if he wanted to see them.

He gave me a blank stare. This wasn't in the police manual. He nodded his head and said, "No, not today. But be careful you don't get hurt." Then he left.

By noon the boards were safely stored in my barn.

* * *

Sometimes liberating didn't work out as planned. I was going down the road one day when I saw an old house with a sign on the door that said *Lots for Sale*—words that I suspected spelled doom for the house. There was a man in the front yard so I stopped, rolled down my window and asked him if the house was going to be demolished.

"No," he said, "I'm going to gut the old place and turn it into apartments."

I asked if I could look inside and he agreed to show me.

There was so much fake paneling that at first it was hard to tell how old the house was until I saw an 18th century raised panel chimney breast and built-in cupboard on a fireplace wall.

"That's a beautiful wall of paneling," I said. "I hope you're not planning to get rid of it."

"Yep," he said. "I'll be tearing down the chimney. If you want it, take it."

I hesitated, but if it was going to the dump of course I wanted it, and I told him yes.

"The only thing I ask," he said," is that you patch the area or my insurance company will get after me."

I went back the next day, removed the paneling and the cupboard and nailed up three sheets of sheetrock.

Four years went by, and one day, after I had taught a class about old houses, a student approached me and asked if I would give him some advice on a house he had bought. I agreed and followed him in my car to the house. It wasn't until we turned onto a familiar back road that I had this horrible feeling we might be going to the same place where I had removed the paneling and cupboard.

It was.

"Is anything the matter?" the student asked as my face turned ashen.

"No, of course not," I snapped. "It's just that I know this place and I thought the owner was going to turn it into apartments."

"He was," the student said, "but he went bankrupt."

Dragging my feet I followed him into the house, then into the room where the paneling had been. My sheetrock patch was still in place. How could I tell my student that the paneling and cupboard were now down the road in somebody else's house? With tears in my eyes I explained.

* * *

By 1979 it was evident that the Preservation Act wasn't all bad. I liked the part about the rehabilitation of commercial structures—factories, hotels, train stations. It was called adaptive re-use—the process of returning a building to a state of utility. Like giant billboards, the restored buildings helped to remind the public that we could save our past. That was important, but it couldn't stop my heart from aching for the misunderstood houses, the places where the dreams for America had started. I was fed up with people who wanted an old house only to keep up with the fashion, with people who didn't understand that a house has a voice, with contractors who were threatened by post and beam structures, with building inspectors who said an old house didn't meet codes, with developers who didn't give a damn, and with architects who insisted that an old house needed redesigning. I was upset with owners whose only interest was tax benefits and grant money, with commission members who didn't understand old houses but were in charge of their life, and with real estate agents who didn't know the difference between termites and powder post beetles. I was upset by the contradictions between federal agencies. As an example, the Occupational Safety and Health Administration (OSHA) had ruled that lead paint, from the floor up to the windows, must be removed and the area then covered with a protective coating. A coating that was so thick that historic details, such as board wainscoting, paneling and chair rails, would be hidden. The same kind of details that the National Trust was saying must remain visible. Preservation was as out of control as a runaway piston.

* * *

It became clear that it was time for people involved with preservation and restoration of old houses to get together: Contractors, carpenters, architects, historians, archaeologists, homeowners, teachers, and those at the federal level who were making the rules. Perhaps a restoration conference where those in the field could share their aims, opinions, conflicts, and technical solutions. I visualized a two-day gathering of thirty or forty people. With all the buildings at Bakerville there certainly would be room. I sent out query letters. The response was overwhelming. No way could Bakerville handle two hundred people.

I knew there were courses in historic preservation at Roger Williams University in Bristol, Rhode Island. I called one of the professors, told him about the restoration conference and that the interest had been tremendous. He thought a conference was a great idea, and offered to let us use the university.

Now that I had a location I needed speakers—a cross section of professionals, historians and craftsmen—those with ink stained fingers and those with calluses. After a week of telephone calls, I had signed up people to speak about dismantling methods, importance of archaeology and historic documentation, grant applications, building codes, wood identification, wood conservation, damage from insects, moisture and heat, masonry repairs, epoxy repairs, paint, insulation, heating, wiring, and plumbing. And still others who would speak about the meaning of preservation and the responsibility of the restorer.

The conference was scheduled for a January weekend—two days for lectures, workshops and mingling. People came from Connecticut, Rhode Island, Massachusetts, New Hampshire and Maine. Saturday night I offered the floors of Bakerville to anyone who had brought a sleeping bag. By early dawn beer cans were littering the floors and the walls were reverberating with the question, "What is the meaning of preservation?"

We argued about what it meant to make an old house look like it had in the beginning. We questioned why a house should be a prisoner of the past or the present when it has a wonderful ability to cycle with all the centuries. We discussed how to remove the phony and how to bring out the best of all the generations. But when somebody said, "Let's face it folks, only a house knows how to be a house, all you have to do is listen," I fell into a satisfied sleep.

By Sunday afternoon I knew the conference had been a tremendous success. The free exchange of ideas and concerns had created a sense of unity, and for the first time I felt old houses had a future—especially now that the styrofoam beams were coming unglued.

Alaska

Talking over six thousand miles of phone line in the 70s meant long pauses and eerie echoes. This could be very disconcerting, especially when I thought I'd heard a man say he was looking for a New England house to move to Alaska.

"My name is Ross Brudenell. I live in Anchorage," the voice continued, and explained he'd found my name in the *Old House Journal Catalog.*

"I understand that you might be able to help me find a house to move out here," he said.

"Alaska? You're serious?" I asked. "You really want to move a house to Alaska?"

"Exactly," he replied. "I'm looking for a very early one. Something built before seventeen hundred. One with the frame exposed and two stories if possible. Do you know of any?"

I felt as though I was an adoption agency. For a long moment I was silent, a silence that had nothing to do with the satellite's shaky connection. I wasn't against moving a house that needed to be saved—but grizzlies, glaciers, Eskimos, and the midnight sun—none had anything to do with old New England houses.

"Why would you want a New England house in Alaska?" I asked. "It will never work. It will never feel right."

"Let me explain," Ross said, and he told me that he'd grown up on the East Coast and had learned to love and respect New England architecture.

"I moved out here five years ago," he said, "and now I need to build a house. The only choices in Anchorage are fast and cheap look-a-likes, built with junk material. I didn't know I had a choice until I visited a friend in the Midwest who was living in a house that had been transported from New England. It was everything I dreamed of. A kind of house that can be passed down to generations."

Trying to be polite, I said, "But there's more to it than that. New England architecture is what it is because of where it is. It tells about the people who settled this country. Without the right environment—a little village or surrounded by farmland—it would be as out of place in Alaska as a Rembrandt hanging in a diner."

"I understand what you're saying," he said. "It won't be in a little village, but the land I want to build on is reminiscent of the East Coast." He described a place with hemlock and spruce trees that bordered a lake.

This was one determined guy, I thought. But I still wasn't convinced I wanted to be part of this until he said, "You know one of the most important things about this project will be to show the carpenters up here how a real house is built."

"Okay," I said, "now I'm listening," and with those words I became involved in a long and bizarre project.

*   *   *

Three weeks later Ross flew into Boston, rented a car, and called me on the phone to say he'd be at my house in an hour. Looking out the window, waiting for his arrival, I was blinded by the rich orange and reds of October. It was the time of harvest. Surer than hell, I thought, a New England house in Alaska could never be part of this. Feeling completely out of balance, I wondered how I was going to handle this next step of face-to-face contact. I had to admit I was intrigued by the mechanics of moving a house to Alaska and showing off its construction, but I wasn't convinced it was the right thing to do. I liked the guy, he seemed sincere on the phone, but my image of an Alaskan was a scruffy bearded, bushy haired, ruddy faced man with eyebrows like awnings, boots made out of bearskin, and beaver pelts slung over his back instead of money in his pocket. An image that didn't fit with a person who would want to buy, move, and live in a 17th century house. But when he arrived and got out of the car, I saw a tall handsome man, aged around forty, with styled hair and a professor's beard. His paisley neckerchief, tweed jacket and brown polished boots reminded me of an Englishman.

"You look surprised. Did you expect to see a bear?" he said, as we shook hands.

I smiled. "Yes, something like that," I said, and led him into the kitchen.

We talked of his flight, the weather, his rental car while I made a pot of coffee. But once he was seated, his hands around a mug, it was time for business. Afraid of being sweet-talked into something I didn't feel sure about, I remained standing, my hands firmly placed on the back of my chair.

I'd already had one bad experience when a client asked me to survey a house that he wanted to move from Connecticut to Utah. When I went to see it, I found a beautiful two story, 1720 house with all its innards intact—raised paneling, corner cupboards, doors, flooring. But then when I learned that it wasn't threatened by demolition, I was horrified that he wanted to take it away. New England had already lost many of its earliest houses and there was no need to lose another. I tried to convince my client that the house belonged where it was, that there were others he could buy that did need to be saved, but he was determined to have this one.

Then, for a moment, it looked like that deal wouldn't go through. There was a lien on the property. Seventy-five thousand dollars in back taxes was owed to the government. But that didn't stop my client. He told the owners he'd pay off the lien if they agreed to dismantle, ship, and re-erect the house in Utah. On paper it sounded like a steal—seventy-five thousand dollars for a completed house. To me it sounded like a suspicious deal. I didn't trust the men. I could tell they knew nothing about taking apart a house and my intuition told me they'd never show up to re-erect it. Despite my warning, my client signed a contract. The house was taken down—chain saw method—and its parts did make it to Utah, but the men never showed. Five years later, the house was still stored in a trailer, my client was still living in the foundation for the house, his lawyers were still trying to get his money back, and I'd been subpoenaed to give testimony about a house that never should have been moved in the first place.

I didn't want to be involved with anything like that again. I needed to know more about Ross. By the second cup of coffee, I'd learned that the completion of the oil line had turned Anchorage into a boomtown with a rash of building.

"The houses they are throwing up are depressing," Ross said, and he mentioned again how strongly he felt about the importance of showing the carpenters how a real house is built. "It's got to be authentic," he said, "not a post and beam reproduction. I want something that's been dismantled and needs a new home."

That worked, I liked that, and by the end of the day I knew that the house he was looking for was stored in my barn.

I don't know why I'd bought that house. I had never seen it standing, only lying on the ground in a pile. The land the house had been on, in Plymouth, Massachusetts, had been bought by a couple who wanted a new house. They decided the old house had to go, but thinking they might use its timbers for a barn they had taken it down piece by piece. When a barn never happened, they decided to get rid of the timbers. They heard I collected old houses and gave me a call. It didn't matter that the house was in a heap on the ground, and that I couldn't see if all its pieces were there or if any were broken, but if someone can fall in love with a pile of old wood, I'm the one.

"We don't have any photographs of the house," the women had said, but she did remember that it was two stories tall and known as the Bradford house built in the late 1600s. She told me that if I wanted it I could have it for the taking. There was so much house I had to hire a trailer.

After it was unloaded into my barn, I laid out the pieces, measured each one, then rebuilt the house on a sheet of paper. By the time I had finished, a perfect 17th century, two story, end chimney house emerged on my drawing board.

I showed Ross the drawings of the house. I took him to the barn and showed him the pile of lumber that were its pieces. I told him I'd sell the house for ten thousand dollars, thinking that he would think that was a ridiculous price for a pile of timbers. He didn't flinch.

"Perfect," he said, "just what I want, and it's all ready to travel."

"You realize there is nothing here but the frame," I said. "Granted it's a beautiful one, but if you want an authentic house it will need old parts to go with it: doors, flooring, windows, mantles, trim, stairways and bricks for the chimney.

"But you can supply all that can't you?" he said. "And of course I'll need your crew to come out to Alaska to put it back up."

"Sure," I said, sounding as if this was something we did every day, then meekly adding, "You better think this over."

It was only a few days later that a check for ten thousand dollars arrived in the mail. Attached was a note: "Don't sell that house to anybody else. I'll be back to see you sometime next month and we'll work out the details."

This guy is both courageous and crazy, I thought, although I had to admit the idea of moving a house to Alaska and putting it back up was becoming an irresistible challenge.

A week later when I answered the phone and heard that same hollow satellite sound I thought, that's it—Ross has changed his mind. But he told me instead that he was applying for a house loan and the bank needed an appraisal."

"An appraisal! An appraisal of what?" I said.

Normally the rules for an appraisal take into consideration the amount of land, zoning regulations, comparative sales, value of abutting properties, and the condition of the house. "But what are the rules for a house lying flat on its back in a barn?" I asked.

"That's where I'm counting on you, Pete," he said. "The bank only wants to be convinced that this is a good investment."

I hated writing business letters; they made me feel brain-dead. I knew I could write about the historical importance of the house Ross wanted to reconstruct, but by the time I had written, "To whom it may concern," I'd bitten the eraser off the end of my pencil. I couldn't imagine what to say that would convince a loan officer in Alaska to give one damn about a dismantled New England house, lying on a barn floor six thousand miles away. I started again and finally, after four hours, I had written nine pages—nine pages about historic structures in New England, their rarity, their uniqueness and their antique value—making sure to repeat the words rare and antique on every page.

I explained how important preservation had become in the rest of the United States, and to prove it I wrote in detail about the tax incentives that the federal government was offering to encourage preservation of historic structures.

I cited examples of museums that featured antique houses. In particular Plimoth Plantation which, I wrote, was only eight miles from where the house had been built by a direct descendent of William Bradford. Then, in case my readers had forgotten who William Bradford was, I explained that he had arrived on the *Mayflower* in 1620 and later became the second governor of New England. I had no idea if that would seem important but it did fill up more of the page.

I told them the house was 24 x 30. It had two floors, a full attic and a fireplace in the living room, bedroom and kitchen. I explained that the house was built with virgin timbers— first growth timbers that had fought for survival in overcrowded forests which means they have a cell structure far superior to timber grown in today's managed forests—and I assured them that these rare 17th century timbers would be fully exposed throughout the house.

I imagined all the things the house didn't have yet— paneling, floors, doors and so on—and included them anyway. And just to be sure that the bank grasped what a treasure this was, I wrote that the parts were so rare that each piece had a resale value far beyond current lumber yard prices.

I itemized each piece, listed its value and included the square footage cost to reproduce the same house. I added up the figures and was amazed to see what a little math could reveal. The value: two hundred and eight thousand dollars. How could a bank resist such an investment? I typed it up, included a set of plans, included my resume, sent the package off to Ross, and immediately called Doug Keffer.

Doug and I had worked together on many houses. If anybody could help me pull this off, he could. Where I was a romantic, he was an organizer, and organization was the vital link for shipping a house to a state that was a stone's throw from Russia.

"What have you gone and done?" Doug said, when I told

him I was sending a house to Alaska and had even promised to send him with a crew to put it back up. Then after a moment he admitted he liked the idea. He liked the thought of the adventure and, as a carpenter, the idea of the money he could earn. Instead of ten dollars an hour (the going rate in New England in 1980), Anchorage carpenters were earning twenty-four.

"Anyway," I teased, "with your beer belly, surplus mustache and chest hair bursting out of your shirt, you'll fit right in."

He laughed. "Okay," he said, "but you're sure he's serious?"

"One hundred percent," I said. "He's already paid for the house." We agreed it was time to start a list.

There were building codes to find out about, a crew to hire, a trailer to locate, and questions that needed answers. Did Anchorage have the kind of building material we'd need—old bricks for the chimney, Structo-lite plaster, white cedar shingles, pine clapboards, and oak sheathing for the sides? Did we have enough old material to fit out the house—doors, flooring, mantles, trim, hardware, wall boards, windows, and window frames? But before that could be decided, I had to be sure Ross understood the layout of the house.

When Ross had left the first time, I'd given him the framing plans to take home, but the plans didn't show the interior walls. Now, before he began deciding where he wanted to put his bathrooms and his kitchen, he would need to know the location of the original walls.

I was particularly concerned about the 'great room' or 'hall.' This was a room that history had claimed as its own. It simply was what it was—a room that a person could share but should never try to possess. Its exposed girts, posts and summer beam were not only structural, they also outlined its 17th century proportions. If the room was divided into a bathroom and kitchen, it would be as terrible as somebody dividing the Plymouth Rock.

I was reminded of a forty-three year old client who had a house with a 'great' room. During the restoration he'd threatened to remove a section of the summer beam, a corner post, and part of a girt in order to install an elevator.

"Someday I'll be too old to go up the stairs," he whined.

"Maybe," I said," but instead of having a beautiful proportioned room you'll have an elevator waiting for you to get old."

The thought made him wilt, and I was delighted when he agreed he didn't need an elevator after all.

I didn't think Ross was that insensitive, but I wanted to be sure that he understood he had a commitment to the house. Certainly if he didn't respect history's features the carpenters in Alaska never would.

*   *   *

When Ross returned three weeks later, the kitchen and bathrooms were at the top of my list. I had made a new set of drawings so he could see the locations of the interior walls. I cleaned off the kitchen table and unrolled the first floor plan. I pointed to the front of the house, then the great room and the chimney area where its fireplace belonged. This room, I told Ross, more than any other, tells the story of the house. It used to be called the 'great' room, now it's referred to as the living room. It has always been a room where people gathered, food was offered and decisions made. It represents generations of ideas and should be kept exactly as it is. Then I pointed to the other side of the house.

"Here is the area where you do have choices," I said, and pointed to the back of the house. I explained that for generations the walls in this area had been shuffled around to make way for a variety of uses—a larder, a buttery, a pantry, a milk room, a borning room, a sick room.

"And now," he interrupted, "a perfect place for a kitchen, bathroom, and even a dining room."

"You've got it," I replied, and I knew this pile of old bones was ready to get its life back. I was proud of this house. It was three hundred years old and still adapting—that is, as long as the building inspector cooperated.

As a rule, building inspectors and old houses don't get along. When a dismantled house is re-erected, it has to conform to the same set of codes for new construction. The inspectors can't wait to point out that the ceilings are too low, the doors are too short, the stairway is too narrow. To by-pass these rules requires convincing the top guy, the superintendent of codes, that the house has historic significance. But how would a superintendent in Anchorage understand the meaning behind historically significant? Ross said we needn't worry, he'd already talked to the inspector who agreed not to interfere, but we would have to comply with the Anchorage energy code. I wasn't surprised when I learned that the R-value (volume of insulation) tripled that of New England, but I was shocked when I realized that meant six inches of rigid foam on the inside walls. This would make the house smaller and, even worse, hide the 17th century frame—and that was out of the question.

"Don't worry," Doug said. "We'll put the insulation on the outside under the shingles."

"I like that," Ross said. "The threat of cold weather has just made my house two feet wider and one foot taller."

But even cold weather didn't seem like much of a threat after I heard Ross say, "Don't forget this is earthquake country."

This was something I hadn't thought of, that had never crossed my mind, that just didn't happen, and certainly, definitely was not included in my plan. And I didn't like it one bit more when Ross explained that the ground on top of the bedrock is a material called permafrost. In layman's lingo that meant slippery frozen clay.

"During a quake it quivers like a belly dancer, coaxing houses to do the same," he said, "but I'm making damn sure this house will not be one of them."

"How?" I asked suspiciously.

He explained that instead of the usual foundation of cinder blocks set on top of the permafrost, his foundation would be fifty-five feet deep.

"Impossible," I said. "That's as much as a five story building."

"No, not a big hole." Ross laughed, and then explained that his structural engineer was planning to have steel beams driven fifty-five feet through the clay and into the bedrock. The top of the beams will have steel cross-bracing which in turn will be the platform for the sills of the house. I felt a little better. Anyway I said I did.

But not Doug. I could tell by the way he was chewing on his mustache that he didn't believe that the contraption Ross had described would prevent the house from swaying, and neither of us was happy when Ross said, "It won't."

"That's it," I said. "I'm keeping the house."

But then I remembered how many times I'd stood in the middle of a post and beam structure and made it sway by throwing my weight back and forth. In fact I could hear my words telling a client not to worry, it's the nature of an old house. It's built to be flexible. So stop worrying. If old houses like to sway during a hurricane, why not an earthquake—at least a small one. And I began to feel better—until I remembered that the chimney wasn't built to be flexible. If there was a tremor, its top could whip about propelling bricks into the air like shrapnel.

Doug, who had the mind of an engineer, knew this could be a serious problem.

"We're going to have to re-rod the hell out of that sucker," he said.

Doug, as well as being a carpenter was also a mason, and if there was a way to keep the chimney together I knew he could figure out what to do. He grabbed a pencil and paper and as Ross and I watched he sketched his solution—a drawing that looked like one of Leonardo's inventions. For the inner layer of the chimney, the part that would never be seen, he had used cinderblocks, stacking them so that their hollow centers lined up like a tunnel. Inside the tunnel, he had inserted iron rods that went from the top of the chimney to the sill. The rods were then welded to the steel foundation and the hollow filled with cement. He threw down his pencil and took a swig of his beer.

I liked it. The chimney would be bolted to the steel foundation that was embedded in the bedrock. It just might work.

* * *

My kitchen was beginning to look like a newsroom. Pencils, papers and coffee mugs were strewn all over the place. But at least we now knew what was ahead. When Ross left, he had his own list of things to do—find out what materials could or couldn't be found in Alaska, get his foundation started, a driveway and septic system in place, and hire an architect to figure out the heating, plumbing and electricity. It was critical to have everything ready. After the crew arrived there would only be six months to complete the house before twenty-four hours of daylight would change to twenty-four hours of night. When Ross had told me about the amount of lighting fixtures he was planning to put in the house, I was stunned.

"Soft shadows and old wood go together," I said. "Too much light and you'll ruin the mood."

"You've forgotten," he'd replied, "in Alaska it's dark six months out of the year."

He was right. I had forgotten how different Alaska was—twilight, earthquakes and the absence of restoration material.

Thank God, at least the need for windows was the same all over the world, and the first thing on my list was to get them ordered. The type of window for a 17th century house is not a standard item. The windows would have to be made by a company that specializes in the reproduction of early window frames and sash. When I called to give my order, the owner told me that there was a long waiting line. But when I explained that the windows had to be finished in time to go with a house that was being shipped to Alaska, he was fascinated and agreed it was possible. There was not much else I could do except put a big red mark on my calendar to remind myself to call him once a week.

With that done, Doug and I were free to concentrate on all the other parts the house would need. I marked on the plans where the doors would go, the size of the fireplaces, the location, height and width of the stairway, the floor space of each room, the areas that needed interior trim, and the walls that would have old wall boards instead of plaster. The house had nothing, and like packing a suitcase we had to be sure it was outfitted with every piece it would need. It reminded me of laying out clothes on my bed before taking a trip to Egypt. But instead of a bed, we would need a lot of floor space. Fortunately Bob was busy working on a boat at Mystic Seaport and the floor of the boat shop was empty.

We dug through my antique woodwork and found twenty doors exactly the right period for the house and then collected enough old floor boards for the floors in each room. We collected the antique hardware for the doors and straightened wrought-iron rose-headed nails for nailing the clapboards on the front of the house. Doug rebuilt three chimney breasts to fit the fireplace openings. We sorted through my collection of interior woodwork to find hand planed boards that were tall enough for partition walls, a newel post and balustrades for the stairway, and boards that could be used for the trim work. Once we had found enough to outfit the house, each piece had to be stripped of crumbling paint and broken parts repaired. It was important to have the material ready to install and also important to have plenty of extras. So we added enough old boards for building things like cupboards, shelves and baseboards. Definitely, 17th century woodwork could not be found in Anchorage.

Ross called frequently to discuss his progress and check on ours. He reported he had hired an architect, the pile drivers had hit bedrock, but looking for red bricks and white cedar shingles had become as hopeless as expecting to find Maine lobsters in Alaska. I never bothered to ask how the loan was proceeding. I probably should have, but he was sending me money regularly for the work we were doing so I wasn't concerned. And the windows? It was March and they still hadn't arrived.

* * *

We had started in November and by April we were ready to send for a trailer—the biggest one available. When an 8x8x46 foot enclosed trailer—its sides painted with stars and stripes—sashayed down my driveway, I said, "Where's the circus?"

"It's right here," Doug said, and I started to giggle. We definitely were a sideshow.

* * *

Doug refused to let anybody help load the trailer. He wanted it organized so each piece would be available as needed. The interior woodwork, carefully wrapped in blankets, went on the bottom, next the flooring and then the frame. After those parts were secured with ropes, there was room on the sides for eight thousand old bricks, thirty squares of white cedar shingles, two ladders, six sets of pump jacks and poles, and the twenty-two sets of windows that had arrived the day before. Doug had done such a great job of packing that there was even room left over— but not for long. When Ross got word he said, "Don't close the doors. I'm going to send over a few things I've had stored at a friend's house." An antique bed, a chair, a bureau, a box of old clothes, a bicycle, and a crate of pottery arrived from Virginia. The next day a hot tub from Vermont. When I reported that all had arrived and was loaded, Ross asked if we could fit in the old shed he'd seen stored in my field. "I can use those timbers to build a garage," he said.

"What does he think this is? A gypsy van?" Doug said with a groan when I told him.

By nightfall he'd squeezed all of it in—twenty-one tons of house and paraphernalia. When Doug closed the doors the slam reverberated up to the moon.

The house was ready to travel with an itinerary that read like a holiday tour:

> Day 1: Departing at 6 am for a road trip to Boston
> Day 2-10: Transfer to a train for an eight day trip across
> the continent
> Day 11: Arrive in Seattle
> Day 12-13: Board a ship for a cruise to Haines, Alaska
> Day 14-15: Arrive in Haines, for a scenic road trip to
> Anchorage
> Day 16: Arrive in Anchorage

I felt a catch in my throat as I watched the house disappear down my driveway. Doug and I had worked round the clock giving it back its life, but now that it was leaving a part of me still wondered if I was doing the right thing. On the other hand, I felt that the guy who had built this house three hundred years ago would be proud to know that it would become the ambassador for New England's first settlers. Sharing a piece of our past could be as meaningful as keeping a house in its original location.

* * *

It hadn't been difficult to find two more carpenters willing to go to Alaska. As a threesome, Doug Keffer, Doug Guest—known as Big Doug because he was taller than Doug K—and David Hobart, planned to leave a day or so after the trailer in order to reach Anchorage when the house arrived. They packed the camper with tools, enough clothes for six months, and two black Labradors—job site tag alongs. The night before they left, we had a farewell dinner. My contribution was a Baked Alaska and when for the first time the ice cream didn't melt, I was sure that was a good sign. Early the next morning I waved them goodbye. The future of the house was in good hands.

It was sometime around mid-afternoon when the telephone rang.

"Pete," Ross said, when I answered, "don't send the trailer. The bank didn't approve my loan."

"Ross," I said, "the trailer left two days ago and the crew are six hours down the road. You're getting your house regardless."

Two weeks later Doug called Ross to say they expected to be in Anchorage by dinner the next night. When they arrived, Ross didn't have the heart to tell them the bank had reneged, at least not before giving them a dinner of Alaskan salmon and a night of sleep. Perhaps the trailer had a fairy godmother, because the next morning the bank called to say they had reversed their decision. There would be a house after all.

*　*　*

Weekly telephone calls with Doug assured me everything was on schedule. Roof jacks were the only thing they'd forgotten to bring and they weren't for sale anywhere. Roofs in Anchorage were simply not steep enough.

By the time I arrived to check on the progress, it was

mid-summer. With a name like Alaska I had assumed it would be cold, but when I stepped off the plane it was T-shirt hot, like a summer day in New England. The tomatoes a guy was hawking in the airport were as fat as baseballs.

I heard a familiar, "Hey."

Doug gave me a big hug, rubbed his new and very bushy beard against my check and lifted me into the air. There was a hug from David, who had shaved off his beard, and Big Doug who, thank goodness, looked the same as I remembered.

As we drove to the house, I caught them up on Westport news, but when Doug said, "There she is," I stopped in mid sentence and my mouth fell open. This was a house I had initially known as pieces, then lines on paper, and now for the first time, I was seeing it as a whole. I felt as if I had just given birth.

The new clapboards on the front wall and the shingles on the roof glowed in the twilight. The chimney was in perfect proportion with the rest of the house, and the subtle shadows from the corner boards, fascia boards, and protruding window frames accented the contours of the house like eye shadow. The only thing missing was a few scuffmarks on the bottom of the new door.

I stepped inside and for a moment forgot I was in Alaska. The post and beam frame, the location of the partitions, fireplaces, and stairway, had given back to the house its 17th century soul. Even the windowsills—deeper than normal because of the six inches of insulation—offered a place for plants to bask in the twilight. Fortunately I didn't have to look at the hot tub. It still wasn't installed. The crew was happy, Ross was happy, I was happy, as was the house, but I hadn't expected to see it surrounded by monstrous 20th century domiciles, or a seaplane tied in front on what I was told was an artificial lake.

The trees and water that Ross had promised were there.

I had to agree—it was my romantic fantasizing that had placed them in a corner of wilderness.

* * *

Now that all its parts were working, I could actually imagine somebody living inside this house. I had even accepted the possibility of an earthquake. After seeing the foundation and chimney, I thought there was a good chance the house would survive, but I wasn't sure about furniture and dishes.

When I asked Ross, he told me that the big stuff, like his grandfather's clock and corner cupboards, would be wired to the wall, and the dishes kept inside closed cabinets. It wasn't until 1997 and a 6.8 quake that the foundation, chimney, furniture and dishes were challenged by nature. The house, Ross said, charged around like a wild bull, but the only damage were pock-

marks in the walls. Like pistons, the drywall screws had pumped in and out, causing button size bits of plaster to pop out.

* * *

By the time the house was finished in November, the crew had been on site for eight months. During that time Anchorage carpenters had shown no interest in the construction. There even were rumors that the house was built with rotted wood. So much for three-hundred-year-old lumber that was 100% more solid than anything being used in the houses they were building. But showing Alaskan carpenters a real house no longer mattered. The house had joined the east and the west and for the people in our 49th state it was visible evidence of a New England heritage that otherwise they might never have known. The house had even become part of the sightseeing bus tours, and on days the sky wasn't filled with droning piper cubs, a driver could be heard announcing, "On your right folks, is the oldest house in Alaska."

Macomber-Sylvia

Sarah Delano loved 19th century buildings. I loved 17th century and 18th century buildings, but somehow I knew that wasn't going to make a difference when she called to ask me to look at the 19th century Macomber-Sylvia building, a commercial building located in the historic district of New Bedford, Massachusetts.

"Oh, Pete," she had said, "it's just terrible. WHALE bought the building to restore it and now the city has condemned it, the local contractors say it's too far gone to repair, and some WHALE members are suggesting we build a reproduction. I'm the only one that thinks we must save it. Could you look at the building and see if you think it's possible?"

Sarah was WHALE's president, a tall, elegant woman, sensitive and gentle with dainty features and warm green eyes, characteristics that belied her fighting spirit. I didn't actually call her Sarah, at least not to her face, not then. I called her Mrs. Delano—she was a generation older than I was, and a person I didn't know how to say no to. So I agreed to take a look at the Macomber-Sylvia building, even though I didn't want to get involved with 19th century structures, not yet anyway. The power and magic of the 17th and 18th century were still running too hot in my blood, but I told myself all she and WHALE really needed was a structural survey, and that would only take a few hours.

* * *

Driving to the city to look at the Macomber-Sylvia building, I got thinking about a day in 1964, twelve years earlier, when Sarah had given me a tour of New Bedford's waterfront—a city, until that cold winter day, I knew only as the location of my dentist.

"We're headed for the waterfront," Sarah had said as she maneuvered the car down side streets.

As we got closer she pointed to a bank, a candleworks, an inn, a whaling captain's house and other 19th century buildings that belonged to New Bedford's whaling heritage. Despite their shabby and bleak appearance, I remember thinking they each had an air of elegance, and I was shocked when Sarah told me the city was planning to tear them down. "Eye sores they call them," she had said in a disgusted voice, making clear that the city was more interested in redevelopment than its history.

Sarah turned a corner, drove to the bottom of a narrow street and stopped the car in front of a brick warehouse. Over the door was a sign with the word *WHALE* painted in 19th century lettering. Sarah explained that WHALE stood for *Waterfront Historic Area LeaguE*, an organization that was started by Sarah and a handful of people in the late 1950s. The purpose was to persuade the city's hierarchy that New Bedford's whaling past and architectural heritage were more important than urban renewal.

"But it hasn't been easy. Sometimes we've been ahead of the bulldozers and sometimes behind," she'd said.

Her voice quivered when she told me about counting houses, chandleries, whale oil refineries, a ropewalk, and a sail loft that had already been demolished. These were magnificent 19th century stone and brick buildings that had been the heart of the whaling district. When Sarah told me that they were now in the process of raising money to buy and restore the remaining buildings in the waterfront area, it was obvious that WHALE was not going to be stopped by these losses.

Sarah explained that after each building was restored it would be for sale. WHALE did not intend to turn the area into a museum such as Mystic Seaport or Sturbridge Village. Instead they wanted a living, working waterfront so businesses would be proud to return. Then she suggested we walk up the street to see what she meant.

I wrapped my scarf around my neck, opened the door to the angry winter winds, and followed her up the debris choked street filled with bear size potholes. Sarah, pointing to an empty lot loaded with brush, paper, cans, bottles, hubcaps and tires, told me that WHALE had plans to move two buildings to the lot. Then she pointed to a building without any insides or roof—a gutted shell that looked like the victim of a World War Two bombing. After she explained that WHALE's engineers had figured out how to build a building inside its walls so its 19th century stone exterior could be preserved, I knew its future was safe.

As we passed more buildings, Sarah showed me what had once been a cooper's shop, a chronometer's shop, a bootery, and a candleworks. I remember that the only evidence of business on the street was a ghostly orange sign that flickered off and on, advertising Schlitz Beer. One building had so many advertisements nailed on its walls—loans, lunch, sewing machines, barbershop, mattresses—that I wondered if they were holding it up. The rest of the buildings on that street and the next looked like they might fall over with one swift kick. But I could tell by the excitement in Sarah's voice and the sparkle in her eyes that she wasn't seeing derelicts, only tarnished trophies waiting to be polished.

When Sarah noticed that my nose had turned red, she suggested we go back to WHALE's headquarters where it was warm and where we could continue to look at buildings from her office windows. When we turned to walk back to her office, we were facing the waterfront. "Over there is the saddest part," she had said, directing my attention to the harbor and the piles of rubble that were the buildings WHALE had been unable to save.

Feeling cold, glum and overwhelmed by the blatant

disregard for our architectural heritage, I was relieved when I followed Sarah up the wooden stairs to her office. I remember how the ammonia smell of a blueprint machine permeated the air, and how excited I felt that there were people here dedicated to saving New Bedford's heritage. But I was overwhelmed when Sarah pulled out a map, laid it on a table, and showed me the seventy-nine buildings WHALE was trying to save. Twenty-three were marked with a star—sound condition. Nineteen had a bold outline—deteriorating condition. The remaining thirty-seven were shaded in gray—dilapidated condition. I was at a loss for words. I found it hard to believe that WHALE was planning to save all seventy-nine.

But I'll never forget Sarah's words: "People might call us crazy, but imagine how wonderful it will be when WHALE has given New Bedford's past to the future."

* * *

And over the next decade WHALE succeeded. Slowly they raised historic awareness, then money, and then, one by one, restored most of the remaining buildings, moved in others, and brought business back to the district. Their efforts were so successful that in 1966 the area was designated a National Historic Landmark. By 1976 the Macomber-Sylvia building was one of the few remaining buildings waiting for a facelift.

* * *

Parking my car in the same spot where Sarah had parked twelve years earlier, I went into WHALE's headquarters to pick up the key to the Macomber-Sylvia building two blocks away. I hadn't been to the waterfront for over six years, and as I walked up the street I was amazed to see the changes. Instead of potholes, the smooth surface of paving stones welcomed my feet. The trash filled lots had houses on them, the gutted shell was rebuilt and in business as a boutique. The cooper's shop was a law office, the chronometer's shop was a jeweler, the tavern was a yacht broker's office, and the candleworks a restaurant. Other buildings were getting a fresh coat of paint. Yellows, greens, reds and band-aid pinks saturated the street, illuminating what had once been a whaler's community.

Twirling the key on my finger, I turned onto Union Street. The third building up from the corner was the Macomber-Sylvia building, a two story building with a storefront. Built by Leonard Macomber in 1816, it had been a grocery store, a barber-shop, a bakery, and a hardware store until 1870, when it had been pur-chased by Antone Sylvia. Enamored by Victorian archi-tecture, Sylvia had added an Italianate style gable dormer to the front and

proceeded to manufacture cigars. But by 1900, the whaling era had come to an end and the building was sold. The next owner, deciding to modernize, had added three large windows to the second floor. By the 1960s, businesses had moved away from the waterfront and Macomber-Sylvia was abandoned. Shingles had blown off the roof, the windows had been smashed, and the clapboards had cracked and curled.

Dying from neglect, the building was slowly slumping like a sand castle at high tide. An arched window under the peak and brackets under the eaves were the only indication that once it had held a dignified place on the street.

I stuck my key into the keyhole, twisted it a few times, pushed with my shoulder and kicked the bottom of the door until it opened. The inside was pitch black and smelled. I couldn't tell if it was skunk, rot or leaking gas. Leaving the door ajar for air and maybe a quick escape, I pulled out my flashlight and shined it across the floor. It was ankle deep in trash—broken bottles, soggy newspaper, tires, food wrappings, boards, pipes, and cardboard boxes filled with . . . . I didn't want to know what. Overhead sections of the tin ceiling were hanging loose—poised like the blade of a guillotine. Instinctively I reached for my collar, pulled it around my neck, then cautiously kicking stuff aside, made my way to the stairway in the back corner. Underneath the stairs was a grimy blanket, a wine bottle with a candle stuck in its top, and cigarette butts standing upright like soldiers at attention. I was looking at the butts thinking somebody had been marking time. But when the blanket moved and a shaved head popped up, my stomach lurched as if the earth had deserted me. Stifling a scream, I jumped backwards.

"I don't know who you are," I said, "but you'll have to leave. This is private property."

He blinked and didn't say a word. I thought about running out the front door, but it was too far away and I didn't want to turn my back. Trying to keep my voice from sounding too shaky, I told him I was going upstairs and if he was gone in five minutes I wouldn't go to the police.

I started up the stairs. My heart was pumping so hard that my head felt twice its size, and it didn't help when I discovered that some of the treads were missing. As I hugged the wall and groped for safe footing, the wobble and groan of the stairway added to my anxiety. It wasn't until I heard a window open and the sound of a body squirming out that I was able to take a deep breath. Thank God the only hazards on the second floor were broken bits of glass and puddles of water.

A ladder to the attic leaned against the wall. I climbed up. In the center of the floor was a huge winch, once used to haul heavy loads to the second floor. The hauling rope was gone, but an imprint from rope, like a mold of an earlier time, was impressed into the wooden drum, and for the first time I felt the building had a past. Then when I looked up and saw hand hewn rafters, I knew this wasn't just any building. It was a post and beam structure, mortised and pegged together, and I felt as comfortable as if I had found an old friend.

My anxiety on hold, I backed down the ladder and down the stairs to the first floor. If the guy was still there I knew that this time I would scream, but happily the building and I were alone. I slammed the window shut, wedged a board against the sash, and closed and locked the front door. I had promised Sarah I would do a structural survey, so I had better get on with it.

There were the usual problems on the first floor—a section of sill, a section of foundation, a post bottom, and a few studs and joists that would need repair, but nothing looked serious enough to make the building sag as badly as it did. I went to the second floor and noticed that the sag was worse in the middle of the back wall. Suspecting the problem was coming from above, I went to the attic, got down on my hands and knees, and crawled under the eaves. It didn't take long to discover that the back plate—the timber that the rafters sit on—was broken in the middle, and when I looked at the front of the building I could see light coming through the corners of the gable dormer. The dormer had to be the problem. When Sylvia had added the dormer in 1870, the weight on the building had changed. Over time this caused the building to twist and eventually the back plate to break. Then, as the back wall began to collapse, the corners of the gable front began to lift. Once rain found its way in, the ends of the timbers rotted and the corners, no longer able to do their job, sagged. There was no question that the building was hurting, but I couldn't believe it had been given a death sentence. The injuries were common and as easy to mend as a worn out hip.

Satisfied that I had pinpointed the problems, I went home to write a report for Sarah. I detailed the damage and assured her that the building could be saved. Delighted that that was out of the way, I mailed off my report and didn't think about it again. A week later Sarah called.

"This is great news," she said. "Can you give WHALE an estimate for the repairs and restoration of its 1870 exterior?"

I told her that that should be done by the person who will be doing the work.

"Oh, Pete," she said, "I just assumed you would."

I wasn't enthusiastic about doing the job, but her "Oh, Petes" were compelling and again I knew that I would have trouble saying no. Like credit card companies, she had the damnedest way of getting people to agree to things they knew they didn't need. I told her I would talk it over with Doug.

After working with Doug Keffer for a few years, I had learned that he had a surgeon's touch. He knew exactly how and where to operate in order to repair structural damage. I told Doug the history and condition of the building and that the city had condemned it, then handed him a key and asked him to take a look.

"You're absolutely right," he said when he called me that night. "Eighty percent of that building is in good condition. Even though twenty percent of the damage is in critical areas, I can't believe that WHALE was told it couldn't be fixed. I don't think anybody even looked. We should take the job. If for no other reason than to prove that no building is beyond repair." There was no way I could say no to that. I called Sarah and told her yes.

"Oh, Pete," she said, "I'm so relieved."

* * *

I was glad Sarah believed in us. I knew Macomber-Sylvia's aches and pains could be cured, but I was bothered by my lack of love for the building. Other than the fact it had a post and beam frame, it was still a big hunk sitting on a street in a city. If I was going to be involved with its life, I would have to find its voice, a voice that was more than its structural needs and an 1870 façade.

I visited the whaling museum and looked at paintings, photographs, ship's logs and scrimshaw. I re-read *Moby Dick*. I roamed the streets and the alleys and looked in doorways of buildings that might have housed a whaler, a longshoreman, a ship's carpenter in the 1870s. I tried to imagine the sounds of a caulking mallet, sandpaper on spars, hammering on iron, the wheels of a cart on cobblestone streets, and the smell of a whale oil refinery. But it was in the next door O'Malley building, the building with which Macomber-Sylvia shared a wall, that I found the connection I was looking for.

The first floor was a bar, a 'men only' place. When I opened the door, pasty complexioned faces put down their beer mugs and stared. I mouthed a good morning and asked for Mr. O'Malley.

"That's me," said a boney, pale faced man with teeth the color of pewter.

I walked over to the bar, told him my name and explained that I would be working next door on the Macomber-Sylvia building.

"As you know, the buildings share a common wall," I said, "and I would like to check out the condition on this side."

He grunted, then reluctantly agreed and pointed to a dirty pink bedspread serving as a door. "You want to look around. The stairs are there," he said.

I pushed the cloth aside. Hanging onto to a greasy handrail made of braided rope, I climbed the steep narrow treads. As if sand was flowing through my fingers, each step took me further back in time until the bar wasn't a bar but a tavern, the smell wasn't beer but rum, and talk had become sea shanties, ballads that I imagined Mr. Sylvia tapping his foot to as he listened through the mutual wall.

At the top of the stairs, a small window cast a pale watery light along a pencil thin corridor lined with doors. Each door had a brass number. When I reached number five I opened it. For a moment the room was empty, but then, mysteriously, as if the present had dissolved into the past, I saw an iron bedstead, a bible lying next to the pillow, a candlestand, a wooden sea chest, and a pair of whaleman's trousers hanging from a peg on the wall. I even imagined a noise like the tap of high-heels as a lady walked down the hall looking to sell her talent. I stepped away from the door, closed it, and went down the stairs, out the door and back into Macomber-Sylvia. Now it was easy to imagine boxes of cigars stacked against the wall, a crate of tobacco being hoisted to the second floor, the furrowed face of a sailor picking up his supply of tobacco for his next voyage. I could even visualize Mr. Sylvia with his well trimmed beard, suspenders and striped shirt counting out the change. I felt connected at last, and I understood Sarah's reasons for wanting to save Macomber-Sylvia. Losing the building would be as terrible as losing a volume from a matched set of books about New Bedford's whaling era.

I was ready to give Macomber-Sylvia a future, except I still wasn't sure how it had looked in its 1870 Italianate finery, the period WHALE wanted it restored to. Given a little time, I was sure the building would tell us, but I was getting pressured by WHALE's architect who kept showing me 'cute' drawings of how he thought it should look. Worried that the building was going to end up with the wrong set of clothes, I decided to have some clapboards removed instead of waiting until we started work. I felt sure there would be clues—nail holes, paint lines, re-used pieces—that would tell how it had looked in

1870. We set up staging and as Doug peeled up the clapboards details appeared like gravestone rubbings; the original tongue and groove siding with traces of the first coat of cream colored paint,  the remains of the three second story Italianate arched windows which still had the marks of their louvered fan inserts. There was even the outline where dentil molding had been nailed above the store front. There was no further need for an architect.

* * *

We started work in August. Doug and crew of two arrived with jacks, ladders, sawhorses, timbers and tools. Repairing the rot in the corners of the gable dormer was first on the list. These two areas were critical as it was where a post, a girt, a joist, and a rafter came together—important structural timbers that supported the front corners of the building.

The only way the rotted ends could be repaired was to jack up the roof. But pushing up on the roof could force the building to collapse unless it was supported from the ground up. Doug placed a series of 4 x 4 posts from the cellar up to the first floor girt—the 6 x 8 timber that ran horizontally across the front of the building. Between that girt and the second floor girt, he placed more 4 x 4 posts. Like a vise, these posts would keep the building from collapsing when he started jacking up the roof from the third floor. When all the posts were in place, Doug was ready to start. With the crew and me standing by to yell STOP if we heard any cracking sounds, he slowly began to pump on the jacks. The roof was quiet. He pumped more, and like an old man getting out of a chair the roof grunted. Doug waited a moment then pumped again. This time the roof creaked as if it was stretching the kinks out of its back. After that the roof had no further comments and Doug was able pump it up to a total of four inches. The sag was straightened and there was enough room for him to repair the rotted ends of the post, girt, joist, and rafter. He sawed off the rotted sections at an angle, an angle that would become one half of a lap joint or scarf joint.

When the ends of all the original timbers had been shaped with a lap joint, he cut a matching angle on each of the replacement pieces, fitting and shaping, fitting and shaping until each one fitted correctly with the timber it would be attached to.

When all the new pieces had been bolted in place, he removed the jack. The corners fit together perfectly, and were ready for another hundred years of work.

* * *

Replacing the broken plate in the back of the building was hard work but less complicated. A temporary brace was placed under the joists to hold them up while the broken timber was removed. A new piece was cut to length, fitted with matching joist pockets and raised into place.

With the major structural problem under control, we were ready to restore the front.

Sarah often popped in, always full of encouragement and enthusiasm, but she wasn't the only one. Located on the edge of the historic district and on a main thoroughfare, Macomber-Sylvia was drawing the attention of the general public, a public that still didn't understand the need for preservation. Strangers would come in off the street, stare and shake their heads. "Junk," they'd say and accuse us of wasting their tax dollars. Actually it was grant money, but as it turned out it was good they thought it was their money, or they might never have entered the building.

Even the New Bedford Whaling Museum, located on top of a hill directly behind Macomber-Sylvia, was against saving the building. It was on land, they said, that could be better used as a parking lot. They tried to stop the work by claiming I wasn't qualified, I didn't have the proper insurance, and that our staging was interfering with a public way. But nothing was going to stop us. Except for the persistent smell—gas, skunk or rot, I still wasn't sure which—we were committed to the building.

Finally by November, when the building was standing up straight again, the mood changed. Instead of criticism, people were showing interest. Some wanted to know the building's history. Others were fascinated by the repairs and often would offer suggestions. We were giving so many tours that there were days no work was accomplished.

One person gave me a 1901 postcard of Union Street. Right in the middle of a row of buildings was Macomber-Sylvia just as it had looked with its Italianate façade—a photograph that confirmed our discoveries.

Even the three city kids from a summer youth program that were helping to cleanup had begun to realize they were part of something important. When they first came to work, they'd sit down whenever I turned my back. I'd tried to get them interested by showing them the building, telling them its part in the history of New Bedford, and explaining how and why we were restoring it. But instead of listening they'd lean on their shovels, look down at the floor, scuff their feet in the dirt and snicker. I didn't think I was getting through until one day I was handed a box. Inside was a brick neatly wrapped in paper.

"I took it home to wash," one of the kids said. Then he pointed to a thumbprint impressed on its surface. "I found it on the floor in that corner over there. Do you think it's old?"

"Very," I said. "That thumbprint shows it's handmade, perhaps even by one of your great grandfathers." The other two boys reached over to touch the brick, then looked at me and smiled. After that day they no longer leaned on their shovels, and for the first time I knew that Macomber-Sylvia would be a teacher as well as a restoration.

But the most surprising visit was the shaved-headed intruder. He thanked me for not calling the police and then explained that he was having no luck getting a job on a fishing boat and needed work. Remembering our first encounter, I gave him a suspicious look. But on the other hand, I realized that the only thing he'd really done wrong was trespass and scare the hell out of me. Since we could use the extra help, I told him I'd hire him on a trial basis. He was always the first to arrive and the last to leave, and whenever Doug or I told him what we wanted him to do he'd jump right on it. Before long I could see that he had carpentry skills and a sincere interest in the building's construction. Instead of becoming a fisherman, he became part of my permanent crew.

* * *

By the end of December, the roof and side walls had been shingled, the new arched windows installed in the gable dormer, the first floor storefront restored, and the front painted.

Macomber-Sylvia was smiling and so was everybody else. Instead of boos, there were cheers and honking horns as people passed by.

On January eighteenth, all that was left to do was hang the new door. The morning was freezing cold and my car wouldn't start, so Doug picked me up in his truck. On the way to New Bedford we turned on the radio.

"Just in. Five buildings have been leveled by an explosion in downtown New Bedford," the announcer said. Then he switched to the weather report.

We pulled the truck over and fiddled with more stations.

"Early this morning while two policeman were patrolling the historic district they smelled gas. Moments later the recently restored Macomber-Sylvia and the O'Malley building burst into a fireball. Minutes after the first fire truck arrived, three more buildings exploded, blowing four firemen across the street. At this time it is believed that the cause was a broken gas main. The fires are contained but still burning."

Gas! That *was* the odor we had been smelling all fall. Why, when we had reported the smell to the gas inspector, had he assured us there was no problem? I looked at Doug and shook my head. Neither of us spoke as we continued on into the city. We had to see for ourselves. We had to say goodbye.

New Bedford's sky was the color of charcoal. We parked the truck and walked through deep puddles, past thundering fire engines, across icy patches, shards of broken window glass, icicles hanging from buildings Melville had known. People were muttering, "This is so terrible," "irreplaceable," "I can't believe this has happened." Some, like myself, just stood on the street staring, eyes glazed, shaking our heads in disbelief and sorrow. Blackened timbers and smoldering ash was all that remained of Macomber-Sylvia.

"Why?" was all we could say.

A few days later, I learned that digging up the streets to lay paving stones had caused the explosion. The vibrations from jackhammers had loosened the gas lines. After that, all it had taken was sub-zero weather, a frost heave to break open a line, and a pilot light in the building next door to ignite the escaping gas.

But Mac-Sylvia hadn't gone down easily. Lying on top of the ashes were the timbers that Doug had repaired. Except for charred edges, his repairs were still intact.

The following spring the whaling museum bought the property. But instead of a real estate venture, the land was turned into a little park—a place to remember the buildings that had fallen in the disaster of January 18th. There were pink azaleas, purple rhododendrons, a white dogwood, and a brick path that led to a stone bench.

The building was gone. But was it? When I sat on the bench, I could still hear the sound of honking horns and cheering people. Macomber-Sylvia was more than a restoration—it had become a teacher, a teacher that had given every-day people a reason to care about our architectural heritage. A year later WHALE's membership had doubled.

House Language

In May of 1977, the Vincent House was donated to the Martha's Vineyard Historical Preservation Society, but our story—the story of the Vincent house and me—starts two months earlier when I received a telephone call from its owner.

"I've just inherited land with an old house," he said. "It's a 17th century Cape. Supposed to be the oldest Cape on the island. I have no use for it and I'm thinking of either selling it or donating it to the local preservation society, but before I can do anything I need an appraisal for tax purposes. Do you do that?"

"Yes," I told him.

We reviewed the ferry schedule and agreed on a date. Obviously the house was worth looking at. It didn't matter if it was the oldest or not. I was afraid for the house.

Riding over on the ferry from Woods Hole to Vineyard Haven, I thought about what had been happening to old houses during the 70s.

I didn't think the owner of the Vincent house was planning to gut and modernize, but moving it could be just as harmful. I hadn't seen the house, and I didn't know the particulars, and I didn't know how the Martha's Vineyard Historical Preservation Society planned to use it. But knowing what I did about preservation madness, I was apprehensive.

As we approached the ferry dock, the engines roared into reverse, then slowly forward, allowing the ancient encrusted pilings to gently guide the ship into its berth. A delicate maneuver full of confidence that lifted my spirits.

I hadn't been to the Vineyard since 1967, and as I walked off the ramp I was relieved to see that preservation madness hadn't made it across the water. I had expected to see a collage of imitation fishing shacks like those of Nantucket and many other re-invented harbors. Instead, the same crooked roof lines still embraced the waterfront.

Shielding my eyes from the bright March morning, I scanned the parking lot. The man had told me he would be standing in front of a dark blue Mercedes. I saw him immediately, waved and walked over. He was tall and thin with a high forehead, hollow cheeks, and closely cropped red hair. It was obvious from his chinos, tweed jacket and black and orange Princeton scarf casually flung around his neck, that he thought of himself as somewhere between an academic and a country gentleman.

"Hi, I'm Anne," I said.

When I first meet a client, I usually use the name Anne instead of Pete to avoid the inevitable, "Oh, isn't that cute. Your father must have wanted a boy." But he didn't seem the type so I said, "But call me Pete," and he replied, "Call me Jerry," and opened the passenger door for me to get in.

He told me that the house was in Edgartown, fifteen minutes away. As we drove down the Island, he explained that the house had been built in 1656 by William Vincent, one of the original settlers. "It's the oldest house on the Island and the only one left on the site of Edgartown's first settlement."

"It sounds very special," I said. I was excited by his story, but I had learned to be cautious when somebody says a house is 17th century or the oldest in town. "You told me on the phone you wanted to get rid of the house. What exactly did you mean?" He explained that he and his two siblings had inherited the house and the land from their father. His father never lived in the house, only used it as a retreat, and with him gone they wanted to get rid of it and develop the land. Not wanting to demolish the house, they felt the only other solution was to sell it or give it to the local preservation society for a tax deduction.

God, I thought, another old house about to be brokered. The same thing that was happening on the mainland. I didn't say anything. I hadn't seen the house, but I was prepared to fight for its soul.

We reached the outskirts of Edgartown, turned onto Meeting House Way, and in a short distance passed through a gate onto a sandy lane.

"This area was originally known as Mashacket, an Indian name that means great house," Jerry said. "Then in the 1600s, the first settlers arrived, befriended the Indians, and moved in beside them. It was a great location. Fields, a fresh water pond, and saltwater coves. You'll see. The house is about a mile or so up ahead."

Except for an occasional scrub oak, the area was barren, swept clean by the wind. It was hard to imagine this had once been an Indian village with racks of drying fish, dug-out canoes, and wigwams covered with mats of woven grass, or an English settlement with crooked streets, smoke spiraling from chimneys, apple trees, grazing sheep, and boundary lines marked by fences.

I had started to ask why the area had been abandoned, when a house spilled into view. As we drove closer, seagulls roosting on its roof flapped upwards, then down onto the mudflats of an adjacent salt cove. Wild grass in shades of burnt sienna had claimed the front yard. A few bayberry bushes had found shelter at the base of the house. At one corner, listing like a passing cloud, was an old cedar tree. Frayed shingles clung to the walls like a tattered jacket, and drawn window shades had sealed the building's eyes. Or was it just napping? There was something about the way the house hunkered into the ground, its steep roof pitch, its fat chimney, and window frames nestled up under the eaves that said history was sleeping here.

"The only way in is through the back door," Jerry said.

I followed him around the house and waited anxiously as he unlocked and removed its padlock. There was no doorknob, only a leather string. He pulled on it and I heard the soft, silky click of a wooden latch being lifted, then the groan of ancient hinges as he pushed open the door.

"This is the entrance to the kitchen," Jerry said.

I took a deep breath and stepped into a room paralyzed by darkness. Jerry yanked on a window shade. It zinged up. A beam of sunlight shot into the room spotlighting a huge walk-in fireplace as if a curtain had risen on act one. I couldn't resist clapping.

I walked over and touched its brick body, then stepped inside its firebox and squatted down to get a better look. The bricks were the color of salmon, and I could see the indentations of fingertips made by a long ago person when he'd pressed the clay into a mold. The walls of the firebox were deep and straight and in the back was a beehive oven— familiar details found in second period houses (1675-1700) on the mainland. I was excited, but then reminded myself not to compare, not yet anyway, not until I understood the language of Island houses.

My eyes raced around the room looking for more information. The girts and the joists were exposed and there was no doubt that they were intended to be seen—the edges of the joists were dressed, the girts were chamfered, and the posts splayed. The partition walls were wide boards and the doors were board-and-batten, all features attributed to the 17th century. Not sure yet whether to believe or not to believe what I was seeing, I hurried through the rest of the house. Like a dog on the scent of his master, I was on the scent of the past.

By the time I had walked through the kitchen and its pantries, the two front rooms on either side of a tiny entrance hall—one room with a raised panel chimney breast, two-panel doors and a summer beam; the other with a Federal mantle, wainscoting, grain painted four-paneled doors and cased timbers—and then climbed the ladder to the sleeping loft, I felt as though the house had offered me a delicious assortment of hors d'oeuvres. Each room was a visible record of 17th,

18th, and 19th century influences, and even the 20th century if I wanted to include the bathroom.

Jerry was following me, enjoying my enthusiasm.

"You know," I said, after we had returned to the kitchen, "in fifty steps we have walked through three hundred years of house history."

I told him how rare it was to find visual accounts of the past. "That doesn't mean that this house is the oldest on the Island," I said, "but it does mean you have something very special. Please think twice before you get rid of it."

Jerry picked up a broom and started sweeping the floor. This made me angry—he wasn't paying attention. I wanted to scream, "Think how the house feels." Instead I took a deep breath, grabbed my boarding school manners, and politely told him that for years people on the Vineyard have been moving houses around as often as they do sofas—and every time the chimneys got left behind. This one, I reminded him, not only has its original chimney but is the only house left on the original settlement. I told him that if he sold the house he would have no control over what happened to its future. I told him if he put it up for sale old-house dealers would be knocking on his door instantly—dealers who were buying and dismantling every old house they could find, then selling them for double what they'd paid, and to people who didn't know that half the parts were missing or broken.

Jerry, looking a bit chagrined, said he'd like to see the house stay on the Island and not be sold to a dealer.

"But," he said, shrugging his shoulders, "if the Society doesn't want it, my sister and brother will insist upon selling it. It's two against one. There's not much I can do."

Clinching my hands to stay my frustration, I asked him if he had thought about donating the house with some of its land to the Society. That way—I wanted to say—the house could stay where it is and all three siblings could get an even greater tax-deduction and still have land left over. But I didn't mention this yet. First get the appraisal job, I told myself.

And I did. If nothing else, my enthusiasm had convinced Jerry to hire me. That was a beginning. I made reservations on the ferry for my car for the following week. I wanted to be alone with the house and quietly take my time looking at all its parts and pieces.

*   *   *

The Vincent house was a Cape—a one story house with a steep roof pitch. The name Cape was given to this type of house after Timothy Dwight, president of Yale College and an architectural enthusiast, had visited the Cape and Islands in 1800. On his return he had commented that he had seen so many one story houses with identical characteristics that he had named them Capes. And the name stuck.

Capes come in three sizes: half, three-quarters, and full.

To be a true Cape, the house has to be two bays (two rooms) deep—a floor plan, as far as I knew, that was unusual for the 17th century.

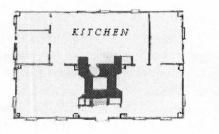

The possibility that a Cape originated on Cape Cod and the nearby Islands in the late 17th century fascinated me. The traditional 17th century floor plan used in the rest of Massachusetts during the same period was a single bay, one room deep house, usually two stories tall.

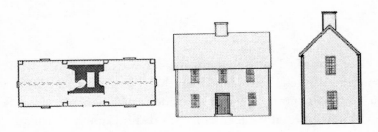

So far I hadn't been able to find out why a Cape was different.

Architectural historians who had written about Capes had only described what they looked like. Nothing was said about the housewrights, where they had come from, or what had influenced this particular floor plan.

There were so many interesting things to think about other than the monetary value of a house, but if I was going to catch the three o'clock ferry I had to gather the rest of the information I needed: a list of antique flooring, doors, hardware, paneling, beams, and boards. After I finished, I drove like hell, caught the last ferry, gathered up my notes and went to the second deck where I found an empty booth, sat down and spread out my papers. When I was through adding up the figures, the antique resale value of the Vincent House totaled ninety-seven thousand dollars.

I was pleased and so was Jerry when I called and gave him the figure. I was pretty sure nobody would pay even half that price to dismantle the house and take it away. But if Jerry decided to give it to the Preservation Society, my appraisal would assure him a healthy tax deduction. I doubted that the IRS would question my figures. What did they know about a three-hundred-year-old house and who would they ask except somebody like me.

I didn't find out what Jerry had decided to do with the house until two weeks later when I received a letter from the Martha's Vineyard Historical Preservation Society. The letter said the Society had accepted the gift of the Vincent house and they would like to know if I could attend a board meeting. They wanted to know more about the house and discuss the possibility of hiring A.W. Baker Restorations for its relocation and restoration. I didn't write back, I called them. I definitely wanted to take care of the house, and if I got the job I might be able to convince them that it shouldn't be moved.

The meeting was planned for the following week at noon in the basement of Edgartown's town hall. The first thing I thought about was not what I would tell them but what would I wear. Pearls and high heels would make me look like a dilettante dabbling in old houses. A pantsuit with silk scarf might suggest that I was a graduate of one of the new restoration schools that give out a diploma after only three months of study. I decided instead to dress as who I was— sweatshirt, jeans and leather boots—the kind of clothes I'd been wearing ever since I started to study old houses twenty-five years earlier.

This time I flew over and Jerry, who would also be at the meeting, offered to pick me up at the airport. Driving to Edgartown, I asked him what kind of people I would be dealing with. In the back of my mind, I was worried they too could be caught up in preservation hysteria. Jerry told me not to worry. He explained that there were ten board members. Three, including himself, were year round residents, and the other seven were on the Vineyard only from May to November. "During that time they like to get involved in a project. Makes for good cocktail talk."

I didn't know what 'getting involved' meant. "Do they expect to actually work on the house as part of my crew?"

He laughed. "No," he said. "I doubt they will even go

out to the house, but I bet they will want to show you off at their cocktail parties."

This was sounding like a social event, but I was willing to do whatever it took to convince them they had a gem, even if it meant dress-up clothes.

As we descended, step by step, into the basement of the town hall, the dull thud of my footsteps on cement matched my heart beat. This would be the first time I would be taking an old house to a board meeting. I knew I wouldn't have any trouble convincing them it was old, that's what they wanted to hear. But if I were going to be the spokesman for the house, I needed to convince them that the house wasn't about a date or a place where a Vincent had lived. It was about its soul, the ground underneath it, the people who had passed through it, and the changes they had made.

I pushed open the swinging glass doors into a vault-like room lined with shelves. There were no windows, only fluorescent lights that stretched the length of the ceiling. Jerry pointed to two men standing next to a wooden table.

"The one with the horn-rimmed glasses is the president," he whispered. "The one with the bow tie is the vice-president."

The vice-president looked up, nodded and walked over. Not only did he have a nose like a blade, he stood as straight as the barrel of a twelve-gauge shotgun and looked just as forbidding. When he shook my hand, I could feel him looking me over as if I were a suspect and he the FBI. I instantly felt nervous for the house. The president, on the other hand, appeared soft around the edges. His suit was rumpled and his face rosy with fine wrinkles like an overripe apple. When I reached out to shake his hand, he grabbed mine with both of his as if we were old friends.

"I'm delighted to meet you," he said, then pulled out a chair and asked me to sit down. As we waited for the remaining members, we chatted about my flight over and the magnificent views of the Island from the air.

Ten minutes had gone by when the president rapped his fist on the table.

"It looks like all the members are present so let's get started," and he introduced me.

I looked around the table. The women were dressed in designer silks and gold jewelry that dazzled against their Florida tans. The men wore gray flannel suits with white shirts crisp under conservative ties. I looked down at my sweatshirt, jeans and boots. It was too late to question my choice. I clutched the image of the house, whispered here goes, and stood up.

I began by telling them how wonderful it was that they were interested in preserving the Vincent house, but as I started to describe the house in detail the vice-president interrupted. "We know about the house," he said, with pinched lips. "What we want to know is what it will cost to move and how long it will take."

I shivered inside—I felt the house slipping from me, its future growing vague. They didn't know what they were getting or why.

The president interceded. "I'd like to hear what Mrs. Baker has to say about the house. Some of the board members have never seen it, and I'm sure it's too early to determine costs."

I breathed in and burst forth with a glowing description of the house and its 17th, 18th and 19th century features.

"But aren't you going to restore it back to the way it looked in 1657?" one woman asked.

I gasped inwardly. This was exactly what the National Trust was advocating. But I couldn't agree. I told them an old house isn't a date, it's a document. The changes it has been through belong to it. Without them, the house would lose its entire life story. I explained that how it looked originally could only be conjecture and as a museum their responsibility was not to one phase of its life but to all of them. I assured them that as an aid to understanding the house I would place signs next to early details or particular areas that indicate change. As an example, I told them the access to the second floor was not in its original location. When the existing access was constructed, the original joists and the flooring that the joists had held had been cut out to make an opening to the second floor. The evidence was the empty joist pockets on the beam at the top of the stairway—definitely a place I would put a sign.

When I was finished, I felt I had gained control. I looked the vice-president directly in the eye. "As for the cost of moving and restoring," I said, "it is definitely too early to know." I explained that I hadn't seen the new site and until work is started it is impossible to know how much repair would be needed before the house could be moved anywhere. "In the meantime," I said, "it's best to think fifty thousand dollars."

But I didn't tell him it shouldn't be moved—not yet—and I didn't tell him that it probably wasn't as old as they thought— not yet—and I could just imagine the vice-president's Adam's apple sliding up and down if I told him a house has feelings that you don't fool around with. I needed to get hired first.

On the way back to the airport, I asked Jerry what he thought about the meeting.

"If you mean are they going to hire you to restore the house, the answer is yes. They already checked you out before you arrived and I know they liked your presentation."

I tried to keep from smiling. "But," I said, "it seemed like only you and two others even knew what house we were talking about. I wonder if the rest of the members understood the importance of what they are undertaking."

"Probably not," he said. "It's the vice-president you'll have to convince. He's the boss, as you might have guessed. He isn't as tough as he acts, but when he makes up his mind about the way something should be done, it's not easy to reverse. He likes to have the last word."

"You know I still don't want them to move the house."

Jerry didn't answer me directly, but his shrug implied it was out of the question to keep it where it was.

"Not only would you have a hard time convincing my sister and brother, but an Edgartown resident has offered to give the society one hundred thousand dollars if they move the house into town. And that's the money the vice-president has decided to use."

"I still am going to try," I said.

*   *   *

It was June when A. W. Baker Restorations arrived–two trucks full of equipment, an RV as headquarters, myself and Doug Keffer and David Hobart—two of the people who had been in charge of moving and re-erecting the house in Alaska. They loved old house adventure and any entertainment that came along with it. The Vineyard didn't have gold to pan or girlie bars to visit like Alaska, but it did have beaches full of bikini clad bodies.

In time, others would be added to the payroll—two helpers, a paint expert, an archaeologist, and a person to research the town hall records. And if the house had to be moved, a house mover, policemen to detour traffic, telephone men to lower the wires, an excavator to dig and pour a new foundation, a stone mason to top off the foundation, and a landscape gardener to plant grass, bayberry bushes, and a cedar tree at its corner.

In the meantime our first job was to perform a structural survey. Before work could start, we'd need to know if any of its bones were broken or what diseases it might have. Whether it was moved or not, these things would have to be corrected.

As Doug and David began the structural survey, I set up my drafting table in the RV, then gathered up my measuring tape, a pad and a pencil, and went across the yard to the house. Now that the house was mine to get to know and to take care of, I had a lot of questions to ask, and measuring every inch of its body was the way the house and I got to know each other. This for me was what an old house is about—a visual experience which, if carefully looked at, tells about old world traditions and the resources available when the house was built. Most of all it was about the generations of history I could touch with my own hands.

And the house wasn't shy. Not even when I shined my flashlight down the length of its beams and touched the uneven saw marks left from a pit saw; or when I ran my finger over the V checks, a carved decoration that sometimes followed the lambs tongue at the end of the chamfer; or when I poked behind its chimney and found the remains of an older firebox; or when I swept out its corners and heard the tinkle of broken glass that were pieces of diamond window panes.

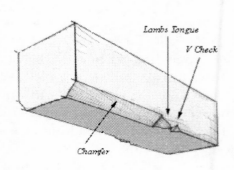

I didn't care if it was built in 1656, 1710 or whenever, only what it could tell me about itself. But as well as the house and I were getting along, it couldn't tell me everything. Pit sawing (one man stands in the pit to pull the saw down through a log, the other stands above to pull it back up) was a method used to make a lengthwise cut before water powered sawmills. But if the Island never had a brook strong enough to run a sawmill, then pit sawing would have been used well into the 18th century and couldn't tell me anything about the period when the house was built.

The remains of the older firebox I'd seen could mean this chimney was its second, rebuilt inside the first from the hearth up, or this could be the original chimney and the present fireplace had been built inside the earlier one. All I was sure of was that the large sized bricks and the use of clay for mortar instead of lime was typical for the 17th century.

I knew, from the many diamond-paned fragments I'd found, that the house originally had diamond-pane window sash.

Although I loved imagining how the house might have looked with casement windows and diamond-paned sash, that wouldn't be useful for pinpointing a period. This type of window  and window glass was used from the mid 17th century to the first quarter of the 18th century. The V checks were definitely the mark of the craftsman, either his personal mark or the mark of his English ancestors. The house couldn't tell me who he was, but each time I touched the V check, I could feel his presence.

Surprisingly the most amazing piece of its past was hidden behind a wall. I had bent down to secure my measuring tape when I smelled mold. Rain had been seeping into the house and like a mother with a child in diapers, I was suspicious. The anatomy was a bit different, however, so in hopes of 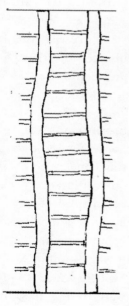 locating symptoms of rot, I tapped the area looking for soft spots. Suddenly, and without any warning, a large section of wall landed on my toes—big chunks of damp clay three inches thick. I jumped back, shook my foot loose, then looked up. Rough knobby sticks were evenly spaced up the wall like a ladder. Because they were held in place by the studs, they hadn't fallen out, but there was a big gap where the clay had been. I stared for a moment then blinked. "My God," I whispered, "this house has wattle and daub." Wattle and daub is an ancient method for insulating. I knew of only one early example—a 1680 house in Ipswich, Massachusetts.

By the time I finished crawling through the house, it was clear that its exposed framing—gunstock posts, girts, summer beams, and chamfering plus the clay in-fill—were the type of details used in New England's second period architecture (1675 to 1700). But the fact that it was a two rooms deep house still nagged at me. This was a floor plan that hadn't become common until after the 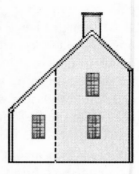 turn of the 17th century—and then accomplished only by extending the back roof of a house into a long sloping roof line that was referred to as saltbox.

I didn't know of any original saltboxes on the Vineyard—perhaps because a two story house was too large for the needs of the farmers and fishermen—but I wondered if a Cape was simply a one story version of a saltbox.

I drew a line from A to B, and blanked out that part of the two story house and then added some windows. It worked.

I had a house with the same proportions as a Cape. If the housewrights on the Island had adapted this concept to their house plans, the only difference would have been their continued use of 17th century construction methods well into the 18th 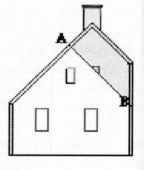 century. If this was true, it could mean that the Vincent house was not built by William Vincent in 1657. More likely by Joseph, William Vincent's great grandson. I doubted the Society would want to hear this. In any case the Vincent House, whatever its date, was the last surviving structure on the site of an original settlement and from all I had discovered, I felt more than ever that it should stay where it was.

* * *

The president and the vice-president came by regularly, and now that the house and I had gotten to know each other, I was ready to use its charms, and mine, to convince them it should not be moved. Each time they arrived, I made sure to have something special to show them: pieces of diamond-paned glass, a 1720 English coin, pottery shards, a clay pipe, an Indian pestle, a copper arrowhead. I'd drag the visitors into the house and show them the pit saw marks on the beams, the V checks, the remains of an older fireplace, and of course the wattle and daub. After each presentation, I'd explain that these things were as much a part of the house as the house was part of the land it sat on. They would nod their heads politely but were more interested in the attention I was giving them—until the day I made the mistake of handing them a brick I had found.

While poking around in the dirt next to the chimney, I had discovered some broken bricks. I picked up one and noticed that the number sixteen had been crudely traced on its surface before the brick had been fired. Later when I picked up another, I noticed the number seventy-two. On a hunch, I put the two halves together. They fit perfectly. 1672. I smiled as I imagined a couple of fellows patting wet clay into brick molds. After every hundred or so bricks, they would have scratched a number into a brick to keep a tally of how many had been made. By the time they had scratched 1672 they had enough bricks to fill the kiln.

"You've found the date stone," the president declared when I handed him the brick, then clutched it to his chest and refused to give it back. No matter how often I tried to explain about tally marks, from that day on, 1672 became the official date of the house. I wasn't getting through. Okay. Maybe I needed to act more like a real estate agent. The next time they came by, I told them how wonderful it was that their Society had raised money to save the house. "But," I said, "I'm sure you realize that the site it sits on is just as important." To make sure they understood, I explained that because there had been no significant changes to the land, it was virtually certain that the remains of the other houses could be found and identified through archaeological excavations.

"Just think," I said, "unwritten stories will come to life. Artifacts will tell how the settlers labored, traded, and worshiped, and even what type of houses they lived in. Bones will tell about the animals they kept, the food they ate, and seeds will tell what they grew. What a fantastic opportunity to set an example of what historic preservation is really about."

I thought I had done a good job. The president's eyes sparkled, but not the vice-president's.

"We want the house in the center of town where everybody can see it," he said. "Not a theme park."

So the next time, I decided to outright threaten him. I reminded him that the Vincent house still had its original chimney but if it were moved I couldn't guarantee it would stay in one piece. It was almost a lie, but it didn't matter. His reply—"Do the best you can."

I was out of ideas. I felt as if I'd gone on a trip with the wrong road map. Twenty years later, I would have had support from the Massachusetts Historical Commission. But in the 1970s the Commission was so new that they hadn't had time to learn what they were supposed to be doing or how.

The house would have to be moved, but I wasn't going to be responsible without having an archaeologist excavate the earth around and under the house before the soil was disturbed by the moving process. I thought of talking to the president. He seemed to understand, but maybe he was only playing the role of the good guy.

The hell with it. I went directly to the vice-president.

"That's not a problem," he said when I told him. "I'm sure we can find some volunteers to do that."

He still didn't get it. I shook my head. "No," I said, "we need to hire a professional archaeologist who knows how to read the soil layer by layer, interpret the artifacts, search records, and write a full report of his findings. If the house is to be a museum, you can't neglect something so important."

"How much will it cost?" he sputtered.

At least I had gotten his attention.

"That's not the point," I said.

"Well, we'll have to think it over. Be in my office tomorrow at nine and I'll give you an answer."

Usually I didn't stay overnight on the Island. I had my family at home plus other clients to attend to. Flying in and out every other day was the most I could handle. This time, however, I called home to say I was spending the night in the RV. My patience was wearing thin and I felt that if the vice-president didn't agree we just might pack up and move out. Then, for a little while anyway, nothing could happen.

"This is a nice surprise," he said when I arrived the next morning, as if he had forgotten we had an appointment. "I've been wanting to tell you that after the house is moved I plan to contact the National Trust. I think the house is a perfect candidate for the National Registry, but I've been told that a relocated house isn't considered Registry material without an archaeological survey. We want to be sure to do this right."

The rolls had switched—now he was the good guy. This game was so unnecessary.

Inwardly I made an obscene gesture. Outwardly I smiled and said, "I'll contact an archaeologist immediately."

* * *

It was July. Summer was in full swing and *The Vineyard Gazette*, the local newspaper, was buzzing with news about the big move of the Vincent house. Apparently we were to be the summer entertainment, and it wasn't long before the locals began to visit the site. Fortunately they were sincerely interested in the house, and when I gave them a tour I was excited to find that many would point to a detail and say, "I have that in my house." I'd already realized that if I was going to fully understand what the Vincent house had to tell, I'd need to see other Capes on the Island for comparison: lumber, chimneys, type of bricks and mortar, joinery and construction. Whenever I asked if I could look at a house, the owner was more than willing.

I ended up with so many houses to look at that it keep me busy for the rest of the summer. I crawled through attics, cellars, under beds and behind shoes in closets. The owners sat me down, gave me tea, and told me tidbits of Island history. I found out that probably there never were water-powered sawmills, and that the boards used for flooring and siding were called 'bay boards' because they were shipped across the bay from the mainland. I learned about an abandoned brick kiln, and an iron bog that supplied iron ore to make nails and hardware. I noticed little drawings of boats scratched into the wood near a window with a view to the sea, looked at old scenes of the Vineyard painted on panels above fireplace openings, and saw V checks that matched those in the Vincent house. I looked for early construction material that might have been re-used. In the cellar of one house and an attic of another, I found studs with notches similar to those in the Vincent house that had held staves for wattle and daub insulation.

I was overwhelmed by the amount of information that still survived. The Vineyard was like a box, and each time I opened the lid I found more of its architectural past. Maybe it was because the Island was a closed-in community protected by water, or because many people came only for the summer and had no need to modernize. In any case, I was convinced that the Vineyard was one of the last untouched places and had a wealth of information that reached as far back as the 17th century.

*　　*　　*

I knew I had lost the battle to keep the Vincent house from being moved, but being an opportunist I began to play with the words "architectural resource center" in my mind. If the house had to be moved, why not have it become the cornerstone for a resource center instead of a showcase for period furniture and knickknacks. But first I had to get it moved. I hired Myron Stachiw, a well known archaeologist, and contacted a moving company.

The mover wouldn't be available until August, so there was plenty of time for Myron to do his thing and for A. W. Baker Restorations to get the house ready for its change of address. When it came to working on the house, no one person was the boss. The three of us, Doug, David and I, worked together to discuss all options before replacing damaged wood. With the advent of epoxy, there were ways to save the past even if only long enough for the next generation of scholars to study the original. But there was no epoxy that was going to save the sills and the joists. They were riddled with termites. Fortunately we found some Island grown logs and a sawyer with a gasoline-driven sawmill to cut them to size.

One stud, in the area where the clay had fallen out, had rotted beyond repair. The original builder had used scrub oak—a low growing tree that had a small but strong trunk— to make his studs. This I thought ingenious because after cutting the trees down all the housewright had to do was trim off the bark, make a tenon at each end, and carve notches on the edges for holding the staves (the cross sticks that held the clay in place). We went into the woods, found a similar replacement, dragged it back, prepared it the same way and, once it was installed, packed the area with the same clay that had fallen out. Normally the area would be covered with plaster, but not wanting to hide this 17th century detail from 20th century eyes, I used Plexiglas instead.

*   *   *

When the repairs were complete, Doug concentrated on getting the chimney ready for the move. It was easy to see why so many chimneys hadn't survived. Not only had the bricks been low fired, which meant they were weak, but instead of mortar to hold them in place clay had been used. It was so loose we could pick it out with our fingers. Still, moving the chimney with the house was our number one goal. Doug had a plan. He installed a series of wood and iron struts, followed by four-inch thick sheets of polystyrene to stiffen and support the entire inside of the flue, then strapped the stack and braced it around the roof collars. He filled the three fireplaces with solid chunks of polystyrene and sealed that with foaming plastic. Three days later he announced the chimney was ready to roll.

Having completed the excavation around the house, the mover was also ready. His plan for the next day was to pull the house out and away from the foundation, but instead we woke to a pouring rain. The weatherman said, "Two more days." There was nothing much for anybody to do but wait, so David and I flew home to Westport, leaving Doug behind to keep an eye on the house. The next morning I talked with him by phone. It was still pouring.

"The hole under the house is filling with water and if the ground gets too soft I'm worried the house might settle and twist," he reported.

Doug was a worrier by nature but I trusted his instincts. I stayed by the phone. It was around one in the afternoon when he called again.

"Get over here quick. The house is tipping sideways and I'm afraid for the chimney."

I got to the airport just in time to catch the last flight and when I arrived jumped in a taxi and gave the directions to the site.

Doug, lying on his back under the jacked-up chimney, was throwing handfuls of mortar at the bricks.

"Christ," he said when I crawled underneath, "this God damn chimney has been re-built, and the asshole who did it used half bricks instead of whole ones."

I lay down next to him, took a scoop full of mortar from his bucket and threw it at the bricks. Instead of clinging, it fell back on my face. For the first time Doug laughed.

"You've got to throw harder." And he threw some more to show me what he meant. An hour later, the underside of the chimney was slathered with mortar and so were we. In another hour or so the mortar had set. We gathered up our tools, went to the RV and downed double shots of whiskey.

The next day it had stopped raining, the house had stopped tipping and the chimney had stopped falling apart, but the ground was like soup. There was no way the house could be moved until the soil dried out, and none of us knew how long that would take.

I told David that he might as well stay home with his family. Until the house was moving, there was nothing for him to do. And Doug, instead of going to the beach on a bikini watch, paced around the house like a father waiting for the birth of his child. He was so nervous I couldn't stand being around him so I went home also.

Twenty-four hours later, Doug called to say the mover was getting impatient. He had another job waiting. He was going to try and move the house first thing in the morning. David and I flew back. It hadn't rained for two days and just maybe we could get this house underway.

When David and I arrived at the site, there were three large trucks, a bulldozer, a front loader, cables, pulleys, people, and mud, but the house still hadn't budged. "I don't think it wants to leave," somebody said. Silently I cheered, but not the mover. He yelled at the truck driver to back up closer to the house and then at the driver of the front loader to hitch his cable to the truck in order to help the truck pull the house. He signaled to the drivers. The house still wouldn't move. The ground was too soft, the house heavier then he had thought—thirty-two tons—and its center of weight was several feet off which meant more weight on one side of the trailer than the other. The mover called a friend who lived on the Vineyard. The guy arrived with a huge six-part tackle to add to the pull. They hitched it to the front loader, added a third truck, and at a signal all three machines took a strain. The house had no choice. Slowly it moved forward. But it would take another two days of jacking to center it correctly on the trailer.

We were ready, but the electric company wasn't. The employees were having their annual clam bake, and the one hundred and eighty-four wires would have to wait another day to be lowered. August had come and gone. The vice-president was beside himself. The Society had been planning a big party for the arrival of the house, but now that it was September the summer people had gone home. At this point, I didn't care what he thought. The house would get there when it and everybody else was ready—and, by God, with its chimney.

Once we were under way, we thought we'd be in Edgartown, four miles away, by nightfall. But the sandy driveway was too soft for thirty-two tons of house and the sixteen wheels under the trailer. Planks had to be laid in front of the trailer, the trailer moved forward, the planks picked up and placed again in front of the trailer—over and over—until the house finally reached the end of the driveway and the pavement of Meeting House Way. It was dark. We parked the house and said goodnight.

The next morning the mover arrived, hitched his tractor up to the house and slowly pulled it onto Meeting House

Way. In no time, the house reached the main highway and the right hand turn to Edgartown. At this point, however, the highway department had a change of plans, and we were told to turn left and take the twelve mile state road instead. "Fewer branches to cut," they said. We turned. The house filled the road. Traffic was detoured and we began the twelve mile trek, but with many stops. Waiting for the electric wires to be dropped so we could pass by was bad enough, but worse were the steel guardrails. The house was too wide and the rails too high. This meant that each time we came to a guardrail the house had to be jacked up, moved by, then jacked down again.

We had gone six miles when a police escort pulled me aside.

"It's three pm., and you'll have to get the house off the road. The school buses will need it for the next two hours. After that we're off duty until tomorrow."

I gulped. Where does one park a 39 x 28 foot house overnight? It was another half hour before we found a space large enough. It wasn't until the next day that we learned we had parked at the end of a runway. If the size of the house hadn't blinded our view, we might have noticed an airport control tower. Instead, when the guy in the tower had returned with his coffee, he nearly fainted. A house had landed instead of an airplane, and for the next fifteen hours the pilots were just as confused.

The next morning the house looked as anxious to get going as we were. Somehow we were able to cover the last six miles with no further interruptions until we reached the edge of town when the move slowed down to a snail's walk. There were tree trunks, telephone poles and fire hydrants to maneuver around and many wires to lower. It was five p.m.. Houses nearby didn't have electricity, utility crews were looking at their watches, and traffic was piled up behind us. We had less than a hundred yards to go when we came to a wooden fence too tall to get by. Doug, David and I agreed it was quicker to remove the fence than jack up the house. Doug took one end, David the other, and I took the middle. We lifted. It wasn't until the fence was lying on the ground that I realized it belonged to the same person who had given the money to move the house in the first place. When we passed by the owner, I swear the house winked, then without further ado, proceeded gracefully to its new location and new life.

* * *

The cocktail parties to celebrate the safe arrival of the Vincent House had begun, and I was meeting some of the Island's influential people. Now was the time to bring up my idea of a resource center. During the summer, I had looked at dozens of Capes, photographed and measured three very old ones, surveyed fifteen 18th century houses, and seen an endless procession of 19th century pediments, pilasters, brackets, railings, and moldings. More then ever, it seemed important for the Martha's Vineyard Historical Preservation Society to establish a center where people could learn about their Island architecture. I could imagine educational programs for the schools and general public—workshops on restoration and preservation technology, surveys of Island architecture, oral history programs, consulting services, measured drawings, photos and maps, archaeology explorations, and more.

Between swallows of wine, I discovered I had an extremely supportive audience—many who even agreed to talk up the idea with various board members. To my surprise the Society and even the vice-president were interested. The following spring they held a conference to discuss the idea further. By mid-summer a proposal had been written and sent to the National Endowment for the Humanities. In the fall a sixteen thousand dollar grant was awarded for a feasibility study. But by November the people who were in charge of conducting the study had traded that job for Florida beaches.

* * *

Sometimes this business of saving old houses makes me feel like a dangling puppet with a hollow head. The resource center never happened. The sixteen thousand dollars were returned, and for twenty-two years the land that **had** to be sold, remained unchanged since the day the house had been moved. Then, in 1999, Jerry and his family proposed a golf course. Fortunately they had waited too long. In the meantime, the site had been recognized as historically important. In order to evaluate the impact of a golf course on underground cultural deposits, the Martha's Vineyard Conservation Commission, and now a very focused Massachusetts Historical Commission, required an archaeologist to conduct test borings before the land could be disturbed for a golf course. The golf course miscarried—the site contained artifacts and cellar holes—and my head no longer felt hollow.

* * *

By the 1990s the president and vice-president had died. The Martha's Vineyard Historical Preservation Society had become The Martha's Vineyard Preservation Trust. But a change of names hadn't changed what they wanted to believe. The brick is still on display as if to prove the house was built in 1672. It wasn't. Or was it? Myron's 1977 archaeology report, based on recovered artifacts and documentary data, showed that the earliest occupation of the site was not before the second or third decade of the 18th Century. That was the site, but what about the house? Had it been moved once before? Is that why its chimney had been rebuilt?

Whatever its date, the Vincent house is still a great example of an early Island Cape. Instead of a date, think of it as a document of the way things were.

A Cellar Hole

The ruins were too far gone to know what the farmhouse had looked like. All that remained was a section of chimney, the fireplace hearth, and a stone-lined foundation.

Lying in the cellar hole, half buried in leaf mold, was a crushed milk can, a rusted pail, a piece of boot, crockery shards, fragments of wood, chunks of plaster, iron pegs, hinges, nails, and broken bottles in shades of sea-blue, amber and foggy white.

It had no address. Follow the path, turn left at the corner and look for the white lilac. "You can't miss it," somebody said.

And nobody did.

It was March 1992. The scene: the Boston Expo Center. The occasion: the New England Flower show.

* * *

"Have any ideas?" my friend Ginny Purviance, a landscape architect, had asked me the previous summer. She and a Newport nursery were planning to exhibit in the spring flower show.

"The theme for the show is Rediscovering America," she said.

Ginny, still undecided on her display, was nervously tapping her pencil on an empty sheet of paper. She had already discarded a Victorian Garden, a Victory Garden, a Kitchen Garden, a Georgian Garden, and a 17th century Herb Garden. I asked her if she had ever walked in the woods and come upon an old cellar hole.

She wrinkled her brow. "Never," she replied.

"Then let me you show you one I discovered in Dartmouth, Massachusetts."

Two days later, I drove Ginny to a spot on Hix Bridge Road where the trail into the woods began. Ten minutes later, we had reached the ruin.

*   *   *

Shiny leaves of vinca lay like a fluffy green quilt on the remains as if trying to shield its nakedness. Building on its slender clues, I described to Ginny how it might have been: framing timbers covered with thick oak boards and hand split shingles; plastered walls that provided solitude; squeaking doors that announced comings and goings; pantry shelves that held quince preserves; wide pine flooring burnished by footsteps; coveralls and sun-faded shirts hanging on pegs.

I pointed to the footpath that led from the house to the well—a path cradled by the rituals of daily use where, even after decades, nature was shy of taking root. I pointed to clumps of moss in shades of emerald scattered about like velvet cushions. I pointed to thickets of ferns, clusters of blue and white violets, Queen Anne's lace, tiger lilies, columbine, Jack-in-the-pulpit, sweet pepper and laurel bushes that flooded the surrounding woods.

Ginny touched my shoulder. "Nature and history entwined," she said smiling and nodding her head.

*   *   *

By January of 1992, Ginny had gathered and delivered native plants to the Newport greenhouse, and by March the nursery had convinced them it was time to bloom. I had borrowed stones from an old ruin, found artifacts for the cellar hole, and gathered a crew to help lay the stonework.

Four days before the March 14th opening, I led my crew and a truck full of stones to Boston. The image of a ruin was clear in my head and I was excited to get started. But when I arrived at the Boston Expo Center and was directed to our exhibit area, I was shocked: a cement floor, a black cloth backdrop, fluorescent lights and a ceiling of corrugated metal. How could we ever persuade the area to be a ruin in the woods?

Ginny saw my disappointment. "I should have warned you," she said. "This is the same reaction I have when I begin to set up an exhibit in this place. But somehow the display always turns out to be what I'd imagined."

It didn't help. My image of a ruin in the woods had already fled—and I was about to follow.

The honking of a front loader brought me back to the moment.

"Where do you want the mulch dumped?" the driver yelled.

"On the cement, and quickly," I said, squinting my eyes so I didn't have to look at the fake earth.

*   *   *

Our exhibit area was half the size of a tennis court. After twenty more loads and lots of shoveling, the cement floor was covered, a gentle hill had been created, and I had convinced myself that the mulch was dirt. Maybe, just maybe, if I kept my eyes focused on the hill I might be able to do this. I dug down through the mulch to make the depression we needed for a cellar hole. After staking out the four corners, I looked at the pallets of stone and said, " Okay, you guys, it's time to be a foundation again."

As the foundation walls grew, there was no longer any doubt about what this was going to be, and by the end of the day the dark and light shapes of the stones had become linked together like an architectural amulet. Delighted, I poked tiny plants of violets and ferns in between the stones, then spread the artifacts in the cellar hole—pieces of blue and white earthenware, a ceramic jug, charred pieces of wood, broken bottles, a rusted axe, the sole of a shoe, animal bones, old quahog shells—things that defined a long ago time.

But that was just the beginning. Stacked in the aisle were tons of plants: native trees, sweet pepper, laurel, and blueberry bushes, a white lilac, violets, columbine, wild geranium, and at least two hundred pots of vinca. For the next three days, with the help of volunteers, we planted.

"Here?"

"Too crowded."

"Move it back a little."

"More vinca on the ruin."

When all the plants had been placed—some alone, some in clumps, some spread out—and when we'd stomped down the mulch to make a path to the well, and covered the site in a blanket of autumn leaves, it was time for a final look. Ginny, the helpers and I stood back, then looked at each other, grinned and nodded. The mulch had become earth; the backdrop, a forest; the light, filtered shadows; and the corrugated metal ceiling had simply disappeared. Ginny was right: the exhibit had become exactly what we'd imagined. In fact it was so real that I wondered if the ruins were the ghost of a house that had been on this spot long before the Expo Center.

* * *

It wasn't the gold medal and blue ribbons the exhibit received, but the way it found a place in the hearts of others. Spectators jammed the aisle. Some stared, some reminisced, some clapped their hands or whispered.

The ruin had spoken for all the others:

"That vanished many a summer ago,
And left no trace but the cellar walls,
And a cellar in which the daylight falls,
And the purple-stemmed wild raspberries grow."

From *Ghost House* by Robert Frost

The Mott House

I first saw the house in 1970—part of it anyway. I was driving through Portsmouth, Rhode Island on Route 114 on my way to Newport when I happened to look over my right shoulder and noticed a house at the far end of a field. Camouflaged by maple trees and thick underbrush, only its crooked roof top and fat chimney were visible—just enough to nudge my curiosity. However, a dribble of smoke coming out of the chimney and fresh tracks by the mailbox told me somebody still lived there. I could be patient. Time would give me permission to trespass.

Two years later, driving by the site on a September afternoon, I noticed that a sign, *Land for Sale*—three large words painted in bright red letters—had been posted at the entrance. I backed up and turned in. A farm lane, its edges harnessed by a tottering stonewall, targeted the way. Tendrils of bittersweet and bull briars spilling into the lane guided me to the end and through a gateway. I stopped my car and stared. A house stared back.

Few shingles were left on the roof, the windows were smashed and the front door punched in. There was no doubt the house was old. But how old? I studied its front for clues. It looked as though it was trying to follow the architectural rules for New England's Georgian period (1725-75), two stories, center chimney, gable roof, five windows across the second floor and four across the first, with a door in the middle except that the south end of the roof pitched down like a visor and the windows wandered up and down across its face as if they had lost their way. But its cock-eyed charm had a flirtatious appeal that made my blood rush.

Picking my way through a garden of briars, wild honeysuckle, and goldenrod, I reached the battered opening where the front door had been.

"If anybody is in here, let me know and I'll leave," I yelled.

Silence.

I shrugged my shoulders, stepped over the threshold and into a small hall. Splintered wood lay on the floor and the air smelled of old wetness. In front of me was a narrow stairway and on either side a doorway. One led north and the other south. I turned south and looked into a room that was two steps lower than the hall in which I was standing—a level change seldom seen in an old house. Intrigued, I descended the steps. The floor was littered with automobile parts— engines, fenders, batteries, oil cans, and tools. Kicking cans aside to make room to walk, I skidded on some grease, collided into a stack of tires, and dropped my flashlight. Catching my breath, I picked up my light, switched it on, and shined it around the room.

A magnificent summer beam reached across the ceiling. Massive oak timbers attached to fat corner posts framed the top of the room. The two exterior walls had featheredged vertical panels with shadow molding carved on their surface. Another wall had a boarded up fireplace. I could even see, through a damaged area in the ceiling plaster, dressed joists and hand planed ceiling boards. Shivering with excitement, I closed my eyes, then opened them half expecting that the room might have vanished. But it was still there.

I was even more amazed when I noticed the elaborate decoration on the summer beam. Instead of the common beveled-edge chamfer, it had a cyma recta molding cut into its edges—a complicated molding that would have required three different types of hand planes. I reached up and ran my fingers over its smooth rounded curves. I knew that to decorate the edges of a summer beam was instinctive for the builders of 17th century timber framed houses, but this builder had taken precious time to embellish it with the finest details.

CYMA RECTA
Cross section

Anxious to look at the rest of the house, I retraced my steps to the front hall and the north side. A chilling breeze intruded through the glassless windows and followed me as I went from room to room. The north section of the house offered no details as ancient as those in the south section. There was no summer beam, no paneling. The posts were cased, and all the walls plastered.

* * *

Long shadows cast their late day message across the floor. I'd forgotten that we had switched from daylight savings to standard time. It would be dark sooner than I expected. Bob and the children would wonder where I was. But I wasn't about to leave before looking at the second floor, the attic, and the cellar.

The hurried pace of my footsteps led me up a back stairway and through the rooms in the north section. All that remained of a yesterday was peeling wallpaper, crumbling plaster, and the sound of broken glass under my feet. But I gasped when I entered the room over the south section. It was an architectural gem that matched the room below.

Thrilled to find a second story to the ancient south end, I headed for the hall where I had seen the ladder that led to the attic. I climbed up and pushed open a hatch. Clicking on my flashlight, I directed the light into the darkness. Its beam, lazy with the dust I had raised, tripped over a jumble of timbers. I crawled in, stood up, and as I mentally sorted out the chaos I realized I was surrounded by roof rafters—rafters too low to get under, rafters holding up rafters, and rafters scarfed into rafters—years of roof lines that told me that all the bare rooms I'd walked through had stories to tell.

The most peculiar set of rafters was located over the south end of the attic. Not only was the angle of their pitch opposite to that of the other rafters, but the rafters were connected by closely spaced horizontal purlins. I was stunned. This was a construction method  that was used to attach thatch or pan tiles to roofs in the 17th century.

I felt disoriented. I turned and looked at all the other roof lines. Which roof was over what section of the house? Obviously, each one had something to do with additions, but why, when a house was being enlarged, would a person leave the previous rafters in place when they were no longer supporting the roof? My head was throbbing and I still hadn't seen the cellar.

I went back to the first floor and found the entrance to the cellar under the front hall stairs. The door screeched in protest, but finally yielded to my persistence. The smell of mold, cobwebs and dampness filled my nostrils as it raced up the cellar stairs in search of fresh air. I turned on my flashlight and followed its beam down the stone steps. Electric wires and copper pipes hung in tangles. Rusty tools, clay flower pots, grimy bottles, and broken crocks lay on the dirt floor. The white washed walls of the stone foundation were laid so skillfully that no cement was needed, and built within them were little stone niches for holding a lantern or tub of butter. Shelves built against one of the walls sagged dangerously from the weight of twenty or so dusty jars of preserves— beans, tomatoes, corn—from long ago summers. Then, as I was thinking about the long ago people that used to come down here, I heard a scurrying noise and saw the tail of an animal disappear into a flower pot. That was enough to remind me it was time to go home. I hurried up the steps and shut the door.

As I drove away, I looked back at the house. I had found not only a rare 17th century house, but one with its later additions intact. Yet the house seemed so defenseless. Would it be there tomorrow? Why had the owner abandoned it? Was he planning to let it stumble and fall until its life was only an outline of foundation stones, or would the house be fed to the jaws of a machine, twisted and chewed into slivers? Or would vandals set it on fire? I remembered then that in one room I had seen graffiti burned into the plaster, and bits of matches and candles on the floor. My hands grew sweaty and the hair on the back of my neck stiffened.

* * *

Bob gave me a welcoming hug, then stepped back and smiled. "You don't have to tell me," he said. "I can see by the sparkle in your eyes and the dirt on your face that you've been crawling through another old house."

By the time dinner was over and the children in bed, I had explained to Bob everything I had seen, and the more I listened to myself the more excited I felt. Tomorrow I would try to find the name of the owner. But tomorrow was a long time coming. I couldn't sleep thinking about what I'd discovered and what more was waiting to be discovered.

In the morning, my first call was to the Portsmouth Historical Society. Located in the same town as the house, the Society would certainly know the name of the owner. A man with a stuffy voice answered the phone. "Yes, we know about the house and the land. It's called the Mott Farm," he said.

He told me the owner was a man named Harry Hall, and that he was planning to sell the one hundred acre site for commercial development.

"And the house?" I asked.

"It's going to be demolished."

I must have groaned because he assured me that the Historical Society had rescued all the doors, a mantle, and taken photographs. When I asked him their plan for saving the rest of the house, he seemed surprised.

"We don't have any plans to save the house," he said. "What on earth would we do with it?"

Disappointed, I thanked him and hung up. Maybe I wasn't the first one to know about the house, but I think I was the first one who cared and I wasn't going to stand around and watch its demise. But who was Hall? Could I convince him the house needed to be saved or would he be one of those hard-core Yankees who didn't care?

My index finger felt like a melting Popsicle as I dialed his telephone number. While the phone rang, I rehearsed once more what I planned to say, but when a voice said, "The Honorable Harry Hall," my words vanished. Clearing my throat, I charged ahead anyway. I told him my name, told him my interest in old houses, told him I'd seen the Mott House, how special it was, and then I told him that if he was planning to demolish it I would be interested in buying and moving it off the property. And when I remembered that I'd forgotten to say, "in a neat and orderly manner," I said that also, then took a deep breath and waited. I could hear the scratch of a match and the fizz of a fresh cigarette as he inhaled. But he said nothing. Should I say it all over again? By now I had an image of a person with a professor's beard, sitting in a leather armchair, dressed in a silk smoking jacket, his slippered foot impatiently tapping the floor while his liver-spotted hand held the receiver at arm's length hoping I had gone away. Instead, in an authoritative voice, he said, "Make me an offer." I hesitated. I had no idea what he might think it was worth. It would be crazy to offer him too much, but if I offered him too little he might hang up. I grabbed for a figure.

"Twenty-five hundred," I said.

"Send me a letter with your intentions," he said.

He gave me his address: House of Representatives, Providence, Rhode Island, and hung up.

I snickered to myself—a house representative? Well, he certainly was that and furthermore I'd just made him an offer with money I didn't have. I gave myself a few moments to collect my thoughts. The name George Waterman flashed into my head. I jumped back on the phone.

"George," I said, "you need to buy a house."

"Okay," he said. "But tell me about it."

Words flew out of my mouth and five minutes later he had agreed. George was one of those rare people who loved everything old. He had a collection of antique furniture, cars, firearms, paintings, and stored in a barn were two houses I'd dismantled for him.

George was under six feet and slightly stout in an old fashioned gentleman way. He had clipped gray hair, brown eyes, and cheeks the color of shrimp. I never saw him without a blazer, button-down shirt, stripped tie, and a crease in his pants. Whenever I went to his house on business, a bourbon would be plunged into my hand. I would sip it slowly, or think I was, until I realized that whenever I wasn't looking he'd topped it off. This made for lazy afternoons, pleasantly tipsy, sunk in chintz covered wingchairs discussing old houses.

George never said no to saving a threatened house. He wasn't an architectural historian, he just knew the importance of preserving our heritage.

The next day George met me at the Mott House. He was fascinated, and as excited as I was. He didn't know what he would do with another house, but if nobody else was going to save it he would. He wrote out a check for twenty-five hundred dollars and handed it to me. I went to the bank, opened a Mott House account, deposited the check, went home, and wrote a letter to Mr. Hall confirming my offer. I even included a check for five hundred dollars to show I was serious.

A few days, a week, two weeks? I didn't know how long it would take Hall to get back to me or even if he would. To keep myself from jumping every time the phone rang or the mailman arrived, I paid a visit to the Portsmouth town hall to find out all I could about the Mott family. I was directed to a book titled *Early Records of the Town of Portsmouth*. The book began in 1638, the year Portsmouth was founded, and contained the names of the first land grantees (land granted with the provision that a house be built within a year). In 1639 Adam Mott's name appeared as receiving one hundred and forty-five acres. Adam must have built a house that first year because by 1641 he had been made a freeman, which gave him the right to participate in the colonial government. But my instincts told me the first house he built would have been a simple one room shelter—not the same house that was there now.

I turned a page. Jacob, Adam's son, inherited the land in 1661, the year his father died. But when I read that Jacob was married in 1678, a date that coincided with the 17th century features in the house, I suspected that this was the house Jacob had built for his bride. I was getting somewhere. But what about all the different roof lines I'd seen in the attic?

I read further and learned that the Mott family had a huge

cast of characters. There was Jacob I, II, III and IV, each succeeding the other in ownership of the same house, and each with at least seven children. It was easy to imagine the house growing bigger and bigger which could explain why there were so many roof lines in the attic. The idea of matching each Jacob to his own roof was intriguing. I closed the book. Church records, vital records, probate records, wills, and a title search would be the next places to look for more descriptions of the house and the Motts who had lived in it. But that would have to wait. By the end of the week, Hall had accepted my proposal. There was, however, one stipulation—after we started work, we would have only three weeks to get the house off the site.

Three weeks was out of the question. Because George hadn't decided where he would put the house, it would have to be dismantled, and dismantling would require cautious attention to every detail, meticulous architectural drawings, and quantities of photographs. Just as important was the time needed to get to know the house. I had a gut feeling that it was architecturally significant and I didn't want to be rushed. I explained this to George and he assured me he would handle it. What he did I don't know. We were given an additional four weeks.

*   *   *

I hired Dick Long to be the architect. No way was I going to be stuck behind a drawing board and miss the excitement of unfolding the house's past. Next I hired Jan Armor, a photographer, to visually back up the drawings. Knowing that the house would be properly documented, I began to gather together my old house crew. Doug Keffer was busy working on another house so I called Steve Tyson, an 'old house' friend and co-worker who loved old houses as much as I did. I valued his experienced eyes and I wanted him as head of the crew.

The first time I'd met Steve, he was taking apart a two story 17th century house by himself. It was obvious that he knew exactly what he was doing and I couldn't resist asking him where he had gotten his experience. His reply, "Right here. It's the first time I've ever done it."

I was surprised and delighted to meet somebody with an intuitive sense of what an old house was about and after that we often worked together. Fortunately for me, Steve worked nights as a typesetter so his days were free to work on old houses. I can never remember seeing him without ink under his fingernails and plaster dust in his beard—a thick red one that I dubbed his personal library. Whenever he scratched it, I knew he was mulling over various reasons why something had happened—a beam cut too short, an empty mortise pocket, a boarded-over door, clapboards on an inside wall. Then he'd say, "I think I've got it," and go back to scratching until the glow in his eyes told me he was ready to elaborate. By the time he was through his first tour of the house, he was scratching away furiously. I would have feared for his beard if I had known the extent of architectural phenomena yet to be discovered.

On the surface, however, the north section of the house, at least what we had seen so far, was pretty straightforward. Double posting, the different roof lines, window placements, interior walls, and numerous other architectural details confirmed a series of additions that began in the early 1700s. When the 20th century building material—plywood and sheetrock—were removed, we would know for sure which addition belonged to what period and which roof line, but I could definitely feel the presence of Jacob I, II, III and IV leapfrogging over each other.

* * *

While Steve and I had been exploring the house, our crew had been shoveling out the automobile junk on the first floor of the south end. Deciding what was worth saving and making numerous trips to the dump with the leftovers had taken them most of the day, but by quitting time the room looked like its original self, and I wouldn't have been surprised to see the ghosts of Jacob and his bride.

The architect, the photographer, the crew, Steve, and I arrived early the next morning. While Dick was measuring; Jan taking pictures; the crew lettering the rooms; Steve and I went directly to the first floor of the south section. This was the birth-place of the house and the place we needed to investigate first if we were to understand how the Mott House grew up. Its summer beam, girts, posts, and paneling were only its introductory act. There was a later plastered ceiling to remove, a

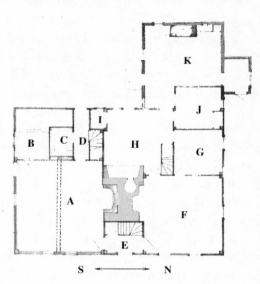

partition—that didn't look as old as the rest of the room—to examine, and the fireplace to open up. That is where we would start: the location, size and construction of a fireplace can tell a lot about an old house.

We took off our jackets and began to remove the bricks that sealed the fireplace opening. As Steve carefully knocked out each brick, he handed them to me to stack. An hour later an immense brick fireplace with a cove back and recessed shelf had appeared. Even though my hands were bruised from the bricks I'd dropped on them, I couldn't stop punching Steve on his shoulder. His beard, now black as soot, made his white teeth look even whiter as he grinned back at me.

"But wait," Steve said, waving the beam of the flashlight above the brick walls, "I think there's another fireplace behind this one."

The brick fireplace was definitely very early so I couldn't imagine why there would be another one behind it, but when I saw a large gap and stonework behind the bricks I knew Steve was right. I yelled for the architect and photographer. Before we could take anything more apart we had to record the fireplace we had already found.

Waiting for Dick and Jan to finish, Steve and I decided to remove the plaster on the wall next to the fireplace opening. When a big chunk fell down, I screamed, "There it is." Hidden behind the plaster was the oak lintel and front face of a huge stone fireplace.

After the brick firebox had been recorded, we removed the bricks. Behind them, as Steve had suspected, was a stone fireplace. Its ancient surface glistened with dampness. When I stepped in and whispered, "Welcome back," my breath, misting in the chill, curled above me, then disappeared up the huge chimney stack as if a ghost had been freed. I looked up. The sky winked back. A gap in history had been closed.

But had it? Something bothered me. If the south end was originally a single bay house, the location of the fireplace didn't seem right for the dimensions of the structure. The chimney should be at the gable end, not on the long side.

When I backed out to take a broader look, I noticed that the wooden lintel that bridged the fireplace opening was off center and too long. Then I noticed that the fireplace lintel had the same decorative chamfer as the summer beam. Had this lintel been reused from an earlier fireplace once part of this room? It was reasonable to assume that nobody would bother to make a new oak lintel if they could use an existing one even if it was too long. But that meant the original chimney had been demolished. Why? Why take down a chimney? Did it happen when there was a need for more room? Certainly the location of the present chimney and its fireplaces had facilitated many add-ons. Suddenly it all became very clear. I called Steve to show him.

Steve, still ferreting about in the fireplace, poked his head out. "What's up?" he asked.

"As old as this fireplace might be, it isn't the original one for this room," I said. "Look at that lintel. It doesn't fit the opening. And look at the molding. It's identical to the molding on the summer beam and means of course it was reused when the first chimney was demolished." I pointed to the partition at the end of the room.

"This house was originally a Rhode Island stone-ender," I announced, "and I bet the chimney was located behind that partition wall at the gable end."

"Whoa. Slow down," Steve said.

I waited while he scratched his beard. Then he shook his head. "I knew you would try to turn this house into a stone-ender," he said. "You always do that." He was right. I was always looking for a stone-ender, a type of house unique to 17th century Rhode Island and now almost extinct.

I badly wanted this house to have been a stone-ender, even if its chimney was gone.

"It isn't a stone-ender," Steve said. "The construction of the fireplace matches the period of the frame and the oversized lintel was undoubtedly a measurement mistake."

My instinct felt otherwise

"We'll see," I said.

The following day we opened up the fireplace on the second floor of the south end, and again found a fireplace built inside an earlier one. After we had cleaned up the debris, the day was only half over. We had plenty of time to pull down the ceiling. While Steve gathered the crew, tools, shovels, buckets, and brooms, I decided to see what was behind the wall next to the fireplace. I pried off a wall board, set it aside, and stepped through the opening and into the space that surrounded the chimney. There were no doors into this area. Nobody had been in here since the chimney had been built more than two hundred and fifty years ago, and when I found a mason's trowel and wood shavings from a carpenter's plane a chill went up my spine as all the in-between years vanished.

But when I noticed clapboards nailed to the back of the wall where I had entered, I yelled for Steve.

Steve was busy sifting the dirt from the ceiling the crew had pulled down. The four inch space between the ceiling and the floor above is a gathering place for things that fall through floor seams—nuts, seeds, wooden utensils, toys, buttons, coins, and all kinds of shiny objects that pack rats take back to their nests.

"Be careful where you walk," Steve said when I stepped back into the room. "We're finding amazing stuff," and he spat on a piece of glass, rubbed it on his sleeve, and held up a broken piece of diamond shaped window glass known as quarrel glass.

"You wouldn't believe how many broken bits of this glass have fallen out of the ceiling," he said.

"You mean like this," I said, holding up a perfect diamond pane.

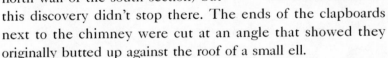

"Wow," Steve said, "where did you find that?"

"You were making so much damn noise that you couldn't hear me call. Come on, I'll show you something even more exciting," and he followed me through the opening.

"Turn around," I said and I switched on my flashlight.

"My God," Steve said, "17th century oak clapboards."

This wasn't the first time we had found clapboards on what once had been an exterior wall (in this case the north wall of the south section) but this discovery didn't stop there. The ends of the clapboards next to the chimney were cut at an angle that showed they originally butted up against the roof of a small ell.

"An ell that had to be removed when this chimney replaced the earlier stone-end chimney at the gable end," I said.

" You might be right," Steve said.

*　　*　　*

The next day, I spent an hour helping our youngest child find her sneaker, so it was mid-morning before I arrived at the house. Steve was on the second floor showing Jan the clapboards we wanted him to photograph.

"Where have you been?" he said. "You're not going to believe what I discovered."

He grabbed my arm, spun me around, pointed to the chimney girt (the beam above the fireplace) and with his finger in the air traced its chamfer to the corner post. Then he pointed to the chamfer on the girt in the opposite corner, noting that its chamfer also continued into the post.

"I don't get it," I said.

"See how the beveled edge of the chamfer continues into the corner post. And look at the corner post. It should be continuous from the first floor through the second floor, but it's a whole separate stick that starts on this floor. Not only that, but the girt between the posts has no chamfer at all."

I knew a chamfer on a beam stopped at least one or more inches short of a post. I knew that in a two story house the corner posts were one continuous timber from the ground floor to the top of the second floor girt, and I also knew that the girt between these posts should have a chamfer like the other beams in the room.

"This is definitely weird," I said. "What do you think?"

"There used to be a jetty overhang at this end of the house."

"Of course," I exclaimed. At some point the second floor overhang was cut back in order to make the gable end of the house flush with the rest of the walls.

This was an electrifying discovery. A jetty, an extension that overhangs the first floor, is seldom found in 17th century Rhode Island architecture, and rarely at the gable end of a house instead of across the front as in Connecticut.

                    *   *   *

Steve and I were dumbfounded by the extraordinary amount of 17th century information still in this house. If somebody had asked me what was for dinner, I would have said three hundred years of history. Dick was just as overwhelmed. For the previous two days, he continually had to go back to his office to update his drawings. But now, with only a 19th century partition wall left to remove in the second floor of the south section, he decided to wait in case we discovered something more.

There were only eight vertical boards to remove and we weren't expecting surprises, but when the partition boards were down and the area swept clean, we discovered scorch marks on the top and center of the girt located directly above the partition wall on the first floor west end. This was important as they were the type of burn marks made by ashes that had fallen through the cracks of a fireplace hearth. If there had been a fireplace in this location, it would help prove that the house had originally been a Rhode Island stone-ender. There was one way to find out for sure.

We picked up our tools, jumped over Dick's stretched out tape measure, and headed for the first floor. If the burn marks were from a second floor fireplace, the first floor fireplace would have to be behind the first floor partition wall. But finding an answer wasn't going to be that easy. There were three small rooms behind the partition. (B, C and D on the floor plan). Before we could do anything, each room would have to be measured, photographed, numbered, and dismantled.

This process would have gone much faster if we hadn't found more surprises that needed to be examined: the mark on the wall of an earlier stairway; a door that had been closed and plastered over; remnants of canvas painted with Turkish designs nailed over cracks; a powder horn with a wooden cap that had been carved in the shape of a scallop shell; a three foot long shingle with eighteen inches to weather; and a flintlock pistol cocked and ready to shoot. Then there were three layers of floor boards to remove. When the floors were up and all that was left were two large floor joists sitting in dirt, we had to admit that we had found no further indication that there had ever been a stone-end chimney in this area.

After pulling out the two joists and laying them on the floor, Steve noticed that they looked as if they belonged together. He laid one on top of the other. They fit perfectly and we could see that the two pieces were originally a single post that had been split in half lengthwise. Judging by the length, a tenon, and the location of a mortise, it could be the post from the ell that the clapboards had butted up against.

"And if the ell had been torn down to make way for the present chimney," I said, "why not reuse a post from the ell to make the joists to hold up a new floor over the hearth where the first chimney had been?"

"We better see what's under the dirt," Steve said, grabbing a trowel.

The room was echoing with "look at this," "look at that," as we sifted the dirt and found pottery shards, two English coins, a brass buckle, a pewter spoon, an arrowhead, clay pipe stems, glass bottles, more bits of quarrel glass, and the lead cames that held them in place. But when the trowel hit stone, there was sudden quiet. Holding my breath, I grabbed my whiskbroom and began to sweep the area. Flat, smooth stones began to appear. After we had cleaned a 9 x 4 foot area of stone, we knew we had found the fireplace hearth of a chimney. But we still didn't know if the outside of the chimney had been exposed, like a true Rhode Island stone-ender, or if it had been enclosed inside the frame, a more common method.

I cleaned up the rest of the dirt and the pile of debris at the back of the hearth and when a one-foot-high wall of stones appeared, my heart jumped into my throat. Here were the remains of the exterior wall of a Rhode Island stone-ender.

It didn't matter that the chimney was gone. I was happy imagining what the house had looked like.

Now with proof that the south end had started out as a stone-ender, I realized that the details we had wondered about—the purlined roof in the attic; the lintel that didn't fit the fireplace; the oak clapboards that outlined an ell; the jetty overhang; the partition walls; the burn marks; the artifacts—had been showing us the way back to the house that Jacob I had built, circa 1680.

While Steve and I had been concentrating on the oldest section of the house, the crew also had been making discoveries. Double posting, and 18th century pine clapboards found under plaster, outlined the Jacob II addition—a two story one room deep struc-ture—circa 1725. Jacob II had not only enlarged the house but had removed the ell, the end chimney, and the jetty overhang.

Another set of rafters showed us how Jacob III had added rooms across the back and raised the roof. Circa 1732.

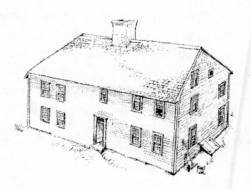

When Jacob IV inherited the house, he added an ell for his 19th century kitchen and that's the way it remained until the day I found it.

"My God," George said when he saw the drawings. "Which phase of the house am I going to use?"

I had been so absorbed with all we had been discovering that I had forgotten that somebody would live in this house. I had even been thinking what a great study house for architectural students and historians. The thought of electricity, heating, insulation, bathrooms, and kitchens made me shiver. I told George he could be involved with an extremely important structure and before he decided anything we should ask some authorities in early New England architecture to take a look. Not only did he concur, but he also agreed to pay for a night watchman. Even though it had been a year ago, I hadn't forgotten about the candles and matches I'd seen. What a hell of a bonfire this place would make, and Halloween was only a week away.

The following day I wrote a letter to Abbot Cummings, director of SPNEA (The Society for the Preservation of New England Antiquities); Richard Candee, architectural historian at Sturbridge Village; Henry Judd, specialist in early American framing at the National Park Service; Antoinette Downing, director of The Rhode Island Preservation Commission: Orin Bullock and Irving Haynes, restoration architects; and James Deetz, an archeologist and professor of anthropology at Brown University. I explained that I was in the process of dismantling an exceptional 17th century house with 18th and 19th century additions. Then I described the house in detail. I told them that it was on land slated for development, but after discovering so much original material I wondered if it was wise to move it. However, I wrote, before I pursued the idea, I needed to know if the house was as architecturally significant as I thought.

I had no credentials and after mailing the letters I wondered if anybody would reply, but within a week my calendar was filled with the dates of the experts' arrivals.

Steve and I—anxious to show off the house—swept and cleaned, then did it all over again. Richard Candee would be our first visitor, and when he arrived my heart pounded. I couldn't stop thinking how overwhelmed he would be. But he didn't faint. He didn't jump up and down. He didn't say this is unbelievable, amazing or wow. All he did was stroll around the room nonchalantly looking up and down. When he stopped under the summer beam and reached up to touch the molding and then the joists, I thought "Great," at last he's impressed.

Instead, he said, "Too bad. The joist ends are butt-and-cogg. After reading your description of the house I expected to find bare-faced soffit-tenons with a diminished-haunch."

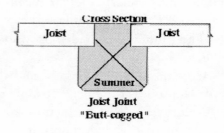

Joist Joint
"Butt-cogged"

I knew butt-and-cogg described a method used for joining a joist with a beam, but "bare-faced soffit-tenon with a diminished-haunch" sounded like words he'd made up. I repeated the words over and over so I wouldn't forget them and when I got home that night I looked in a book I

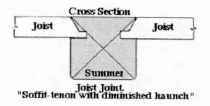

had about the development of carpentry. There were such words. After reading the description, I understood why he wanted to examine the end of the joists. Bare-faced soffit-tenon with diminished-haunch (today referred to as tusk tenon) was a carpentry joint used by the earliest settlers which, if he had seen it, would have suggested that the house had been constructed before 1680. On the other hand, a butt and cog joint, a more economical method of carpentry, was often found in New England houses constructed after 1680. But I wouldn't know that until the evening. In the mean time, I suspected that Candee was hoping that the house was earlier than it was.

Perhaps Candee hoped the house was earlier than it was, but certainly when he got to the second floor and saw the oak clapboards, the burn marks in the girt, the evidence of a jetty overhang, he'd be impressed. Instead he nodded his head as if he had seen it all before, and I found myself questioning if the house was as special as I thought. But when we got to the attic and he saw the roof with the purlins, he grabbed his forehead, drew in his breath, and said, "Superior." The word I'd been waiting to hear.

The Mott House had spoken to him as it would to many others.

Cummings, Judd, Haynes and Bullock reported that the Mott House was the finest example of unspoiled 17th century architecture in Rhode Island—an amazing find and key document in the development of 17th century vernacular architecture. And they confirmed that it should not be moved. Downing, although she didn't go past the front hall, agreed with what everybody else had said

But the most extraordinary visitor was Jim Deetz. As I watched him unwind his long-legged frame from his truck, I knew I was going to like him. His wiry sideburns outlined a ruggedly handsome face, and instead of a suit and tie he was wearing a faded jean jacket, a cowboy hat, boots, and a leather belt with a large topaz and silver buckle.

"I've been looking forward to seeing this place," he said, as his rough hand took hold of mine and gave it a shake.

"Does all this acreage belong with the house?" he asked. His eyes drifted from the house to the outbuildings, down a lane, across yellow fields of goldenrod to the shores of Narragansett Bay.

"Yes," I said. "In fact this is the original one hundred and forty acres that was granted to Adam Mott in 1639." I pointed to the south end of the house and told him it had been built around 1680 by Adam's son.

"Let's have a look," he said.

Jim's words, "superb, splendid, wonderful," followed me as I led him from room to room—words that included all the additions, which surprised me as I hadn't thought of them as architecturally significant.

"You've got everything here," he said. "An original farm site, three hundred years of habitation, and a structure that holds a wealth of cultural and social information."

He explained that the construction of the south end—exposed and chamfered frame, end chimney, jetty overhang, studded walls, casement windows—shows that the builder, Jacob I, in 1680 still had strong ties to the post-medieval architecture of Old England while the first addition indicates that the builder, Jacob II, was responding to the architectural influences taking place in New England and particularly Rhode Island.

"He was becoming Americanized," Jim said and clarified

his statement by pointing out that Jacob II had framed the walls of his addition with planks instead of studs, his windows were double-hung instead of casement, and rather than leaving the timbers exposed he had cased the posts and hidden the summer, the girts and the joists under a plaster ceiling, just as his neighbors were doing.

"But that is only part of it," Jim said and proceeded to explain that when Jacob II removed the jetty, replaced the end chimney with a center one, added five windows across the front, and moved the door to the middle, it wasn't only a change in style and details but a change from the old-world asymmetric tradition of building to the new world of symmetry, the hallmark of the Georgian period.

"Except," Jim continued, "Jacob II didn't understand the architectural rules for symmetry. He placed the sills for his addition one foot higher than the sills of the original house, a design mistake that would mean the windows on the front could never be symmetrical."

"That's why the front of the house looks so out of sync," I said.

"Yes," Jim said. He explained that by the time Jacob III inherited the house, the Georgian period would have been in full swing. Wanting his house to look like those in the center of town, he added rooms across the back and raised the roof so the peak would be parallel with the front.

"Poor Jacob," I said. "As hard as he tried to make his house look Georgian, he was stuck with the two different levels. Then when he decided to raise the roof, the original 17th century roof was at right angles to his new roof, and in the way.

"Right," Jim said. "He couldn't remove it as it was structurally part of the south end."

The best Jacob III could do, Jim explained, was to hide the north slant of the 17th century roof under his new roof while hoping that the south slant mirrored the hip roofs that had become fashionable in next-door Newport.

"And the neighbors would know he was one of them," I said.

"Yes, and it's clear that mattered to the Motts. Here's a good example," he said, as he picked out a fragment of painted canvas from the basket of artifacts. Holding it up, he told me that at one time it was fashionable to cover a table with a Turkish carpet from the East, but the Motts probably couldn't afford the real thing so they used an imitation—canvas painted with an eastern design.

Jim had been showing me a whole new way to look at a house, and by the time we had finished the tour the Motts had become real people instead of roof lines, additions and a basket of artifacts.

"I suspect that you know this house and site are extremely important," Jim said as we walked back to his truck. "To find a 1639 allotment of land and a three hundred year old house passed down in the same family with all its changes intact is unique in Colonial America. Not just the house but the entire site needs to be studied."

And he talked excitedly about core samples, test pits, looking for cellar holes, privies, wells, plus researching deeds, wills, probate, and church records.

"But first while the house is still on site it is critical to investigate the soil under the first floor," he said. "That way we can study how the artifacts relate to the standing structure and hence the life ways of those that lived in the house."

*   *   *

George seldom visited the house. He lived an hour away and preferred getting updates by phone. When I called to tell him about Jim's visit, he was fascinated and definitely wanted archaeological research on the house before it was taken down. But Jim wasn't free until January, well past our agreed upon time to have the house out of there. George wrote a letter to Hall. He asked for an extension and included an article the local newspaper had written titled, *300 Years of History found in One House.*

Hall couldn't say no. He admitted to George that he had no plans to do anything with the site for another year.

A year!

The words that I had been hearing reeled around in my head: "It's too important to move; should be kept on the site; a key document of the social and cultural changes that took place in New England."

Could we keep the house on the site? Could it be used as an architectural museum/study center? Could we raise enough money to buy the land?

The experts who had seen the house said, "Yes," and agreed to help.

But what about George? His expenses (the purchase, the architect, the photographer, the watchman, the crew, and Steve and myself) already exceeded twenty thousand and he still didn't have his house. Would he be willing to give it up?

George continued to amaze me. "If the Mott House is that important," he said, "it should belong to people, not an individual."

It helped that we had discovered that Mary Mott, the mother of Major General Nathanael Greene, Revolutionary War hero, was also George's ancestress, and that George Fox, the founder of the Society of Friends, or Quakers, had preached in the house in the late1600s.

Steve was excited. He felt as strongly as I did that we were involved with something rare and unique. "But how are you going to buy the land?" he asked.

"Meetings," I said. And we boarded up the windows and doors.

The first step had been accomplished. The next step was to raise the five hundred thousand that Hall was asking for the property, then convince the public of the importance of saving the house.

The meetings began. Antoinette Downing would do the necessary paperwork to get the site on the National Registry and explore various ways to keep the house on the site. The experts would solicit organizations. I would solicit individuals. Letters were written, phone calls made, newspaper articles written. The interest grew. But Downing, who had taken charge, kept turning potential sources down, for there always seemed to be another and better option for land acquisition. When one didn't come through, she said she knew of another. The house had become a pawn in a chess game. Months went by, and the only person who accomplished anything was Jim Deetz, who managed to get a grant that would pay for a summer dig inside and around the perimeter of the house.

George was losing interest. After six months, there was still no plan for a way to preserve the Mott House on site.

"So many people are involved in this," he said. "But nobody has come through. I can't really wait forever." He declared August to be the deadline.

I agreed. I was frustrated by all the complex dealings and worried about the house itself: open to the weather, it had been stripped of shingles, plaster, lath: all the things that help a building stay dry and standing. I had an ominous feeling that if something wasn't decided soon it might collapse.

All it took was hearing ideas about yet another scheme and another year to develop it, to make me phone George. "I'm calling the crew back," I announced. "We're taking the Mott House down."

None of us had been in a position to take care of it where it was. Steve and I were sad, but we knew dismantling the house was the next best thing for its future. Anyway it still had things to show us. As it came down, we were able to examine, measure and record all its joinery methods, details that otherwise would never have been revealed.

*　*　*

The trailer holding the house followed me as I led it to George's place. The Mott House's pilgrimage over, we gently unloaded its parts into his barn. George planned to re-assemble it within a year. But one year, then two, and then a third went by until finally one day George called. "I'm selling my place in Rhode Island and moving to Vermont. I can't use the house. Can you sell it?"

I found a prospective buyer and brought him to see the disassembled Mott House. But when I opened up the barn where it was stored, a stifling smell of decay rushed by me. The doors and the windows of the barn had been closed for three years, and the building, unable to breath, had suffocated. I bent down and touched the summer beam, the backbone of the house. It crumbled in my hand.

*   *   *

Thirty years later, the stonewalls, fields of goldenrod, winding lanes, and gnarled fruit trees have been replaced by checkerboard lots and houses that look as if they came out of a box. I often wonder what owners think when they find a rusted hinge, an axe head, a horseshoe, an iron lock, a pipe stem, while they dig in their gardens. Do they know that they are living on land that once was the site of a Rhode Island stone-ender–The Mott House—the last of its kind?

Epilogue

My children are all grown up now. Although none of them have become an old house fanatics like their mother, at least not yet, they each have become expert in their own field.

My oldest is a film producer, the next an historian, the third a computer engineer, the forth a carpenter, the fifth an interior designer, the sixth a yacht captain, and the seventh a massage practitioner.

Bob, my soul mate, wasn't so lucky. He promised me he'd live to be ninety—instead, in 1983 at the age of fifty-six, he died from a brain tumor. But I know that everything I do each day has his blessings . . . . well . . . . maybe not everything, but almost.

And my grandmother's house, the first old house that opened its arms to me, is being lovingly taken care of by my ex-husband's ex-wife. The next owners will be my children. Undoubtedly when that time comes, they too will be bewitched by the magic of a 17th century structure.

*   *   *

And me? It's 2003 and yes, I'm as deeply into old structures as ever. There is still so much to learn and so much to see. It's true that today there are few early houses to discover, but examining the ones that have survived, or ones that other architectural historians have seen, is to discover the construction methods and decorative features I haven't seen—even when it means using a powerful magnifying glass to look for 17th and 18th century architectural details in 19th century photographs.

Every old house has a story—in its cellar, attic, and behind its walls: imprints from hinges, latches, locks and window catches; a lambs tongue at the end of a chamfer; the chafe marks from daily chores and thresholds worn from years of footsteps; a broken saucer, a pewter spoon, an English coin; and the carpenter's scribe marks and Roman numerals that link a house to the day of raising.

Thus in each ancient structure there are clues to the past—if we take the time and concern to look, to learn, to touch, to document, to preserve. By so doing we will be able to give our past to the future.

So simple and so essential.

Pete Baker, Westport, 2003

Appendix

This drawing is typical of post and beam framing used in New England during the 17th and 18th century. Whether a two story, one bay deep house with a center chimney like this drawing, or a one story house, a house with an end chimney, or a house that is two bays deep, the method for framing was basically the same.

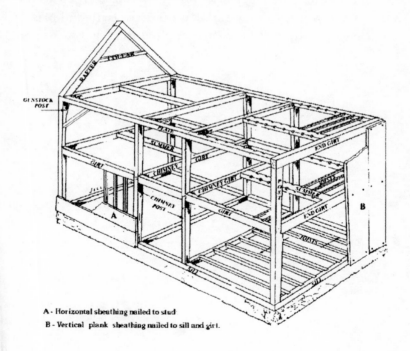

A - Horizontal sheathing nailed to stud
B - Vertical plank sheathing nailed to sill and girt.

The posts and girts average 7x8 inches in size and the summer beam 10x11 inches. Hardwood such as oak and chestnut was the favored wood, but it is not uncommon to find hard pine, hemlock, spruce, and poplar.

Either studs or wide boards called planks were used for the vertical support of the walls.

If studs were used **(A)** their ends were framed into the sill and girt by means of a mortise and tenon. This meant that the studs had to be put in place as the house was raised. After the frame was standing, either horizontal boards or clapboards were nailed to the outside surface and lath and plaster was applied to their inside edge. This left a four inch gap between the outside and inside wall, an area that sometimes was filled with bricks—insulation yes, but for sure it helped to keep the rats out.

When vertical planking **(B)** was used—oak boards, often one and one-half inches thick were nailed or pegged to the sill, girt and plate after the frame was raised. Lath and plaster or a coat of whitewash was then applied directly on to their inside surface.

Glossary

Baseboard: The board at the bottom of a plastered wall.

Baluster: A turned or rectangular upright supporting a stair rail.

Beaded: A half round molding cut into a board vertically.

Brace: Diagonal timber placed between two beams to strengthen the frame.

Came: An **H** shaped lead strip that holds window glass.

Cased: Boards nailed over the interior framing beams. 18th century.

Chamfer: A bevel or slope cut on the inner edges of framing timbers to take off the sharp corner.

Chamfer stop: A way of bringing the chamfer to an end before a beam meets another beam.

Chimney breast: A paneled wall over the fireplace.

Casement: A window hinged to swing outward.

Closed string: When the stair tread ends are behind a board and cannot be seen.

Collar: A beam that holds the rafters apart to divert lateral pressure.

Corner post: See *Post*

Dentil molding: Small blocks in a  cornice.

Dressed: A rough timber that has been planed smooth.

Dutchman: A repair to a damaged piece of wood.

Eave: Projected edge of a roof.

Ell: A small one or one and a half story building attached to a house.

Exposed frame: The framing timbers visible on the inside of a house. Not cased. See *Case*.

Fascia: A flat band of wood.

Featheredged boards: A feathered or tapered board inserted into a groove on another board.

Firebox: The fireplace.

Gable end: The wall end between two slopes of a roof.

Gable roof: A roof with a single slope on each side.

Gambrel: A roof with two slopes on each side.

Girt: A beam framed into the corner posts of a framed building.

Gunstock post: A projection at the head of a post to enlarge the bea-ring space. Often referred to as bracketed or splayed.

H hinge: An 18th century wrought-iron door hinge.

HL hinge: An 18th century wrought-iron door hinge.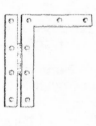

Top and bottom hinge.

Hewn: A timber that has been shaped with an axe.

Jetty: A wall projecting over one beneath.

Joist: A smaller beam that supports the floor boards.

Lambs tongue: A decorative molding often used for the chamfer stop.

Lean-to: A structure with a single-pitch roof that is attached to the side of a building as an extension.

Lights: The panes of glass in a window.

Lintel: A heavy beam of stone or wood bridging an opening.

Mortise: A rectangular cut-out in a beam to receive a tenon. See *Tenon*

Over-mantle: See *Chimney breast.*

Paneling: Panels set into stiles (vertical strips of wood) and rails (horizontal strips of wood).

Pilaster: A projected mass as an ornamental motif.

Plate: The beam framed on the top of the posts that carries the rafters.

Planking: Vertical boards, usually oak, that span the area from the sill to the plate

Post: A vertical timber that carries the girts and the plates.

Purlins: Longitudinal timbers laid across the rafters.

Quarrel glass: A diamond shaped piece of window glass set into place with lead *cames.*

Rafter: The beam forming the slope of a roof.

Ridge: The peak of a roof.

Riven: Wood split with the grain; such as clapboards, shingles, laths.

Scarf joint: A joint used to join two beams.

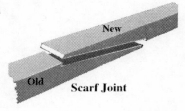

New

Old Scarf Joint

Shadow molding: Molding cut into the surface of wall boards to create shadows. Jacobean in nature.

Sheathing: Boards, unusually oak, set vertically, or horizontally when a house is studded.

Ship-lapped: Floor boards joined with a lap.

Single bay: A one room deep house.

Soffit: The underside of a structural or decorative component.

Sill: Horizontal beam laid directly on the foundation from which the frame work of a building is erected.

Stud: A vertical beam used in the outside wall or partitions of a wood framed structure.

Summer beam: The beam in the center of a ceiling that carries the joists for the floor above.

Tenon: A projection cut at the end of a beam to fit into a mortise. See Mortice.

Thatch: Coarse grass sometimes used for roofing in the 17th century.

Triple turn stairway: Stairway that has three turns between floors.

Wainscoting: Horizontal boards or paneling covering the lower section of interior walls.

Recommended Bibliography

Early Rhode Island Houses—Norman Isham and Albert Brown, Preston and Rounds, 1895. A wonderful study of R.I. houses from 36 to 1725. The text is crystal clear and there are excellent illustrations. An important book.

The Framed Houses of Massachusetts Bay, 1625-1725—Abbott Lowell Cummings, Harvard University Press, 1979.
A study of Massachusetts Bay's early houses. With photos and illustrations, and an extensive research of colonial records. A must.

In Small Things Forgotten—James Deetz, Doubleday, 1977.
Excellent description of the Mott House.

Among Friends—Marley Brown III, University of Michigan, 1987.
The archaeological investigation at Mott Farm.

Early Homes of Rhode Island – Antoinette F. Downing, Garrett and Massie, 1937.
An historical record of the development of Rhode Island architecture.

Early Connecticut Houses—Norman Isham and Albert Brown, Dover Publications, 1965.
Excellent study of Connecticut Houses from 1635 to 1750.

Architectural Changes in Colonial Rhode Island—Dell Upton, Society of the Preservation of New England Antiquities, 1979.
> A case study of the Mott House.

The Development of Carpentry 1200-1700—Cecil Alex Hewett, Augustus M. Keller Publishers, 1969.
> The history of framing-joints with excellent illustrations.

The Beam Framing Book—Stewart Elliott and Eugenie Wallas, Housesmiths Press, 1977.
> How to build a beam framed house.

Early Domestic Architecture of Connecticut—J. Frederick Kelly, Dover Publications, N.Y. 1963.
> Rich in architectural drawings and text.

The Vincent House—A.W. Baker, Dukes County Historical Society, 1978.
> An architectural description of the Vincent House.